The Limits of Humanitarian Intervention

ALAN J. KUPERMAN

THE LIMITS OF HUMANITARIAN INTERVENTION

Genocide in Rwanda

BROOKINGS INSTITUTION PRESS
Washington, D.C.

Copyright © 2001
THE BROOKINGS INSTITUTION
1775 Massachusetts Avenue, N.W., Washington, D.C. 20036
www.brookings.edu

Library of Congress Cataloging-in-Publication data
Kuperman, Alan J.
  The limits of humanitarian intervention : genocide in Rwanda / Alan J. Kuperman.
    p.   cm.
Includes bibliographical references (p.) and index.
  ISBN 0-8157-0086-5 (alk. paper)
  ISBN 0-8157-0085-7 (pbk. : alk. paper)
  1. Rwanda—History—Civil War, 1994—Atrocities. 2. Genocide—
Rwanda—History-20th century. 3. Rwanda—Ethnic relations. 4. Tutsi (African people)—Crimes against—Rwanda—History—20th century. 5. Hutu (African people)—Rwanda—Politics and government—20th century. 6. Humanitarian intervention—Rwanda—History—20th century. 7. United Nations—Rwanda. I. Title.

DT450.435 .K86 2001   2001000441
967.57104—dc21   CIP

9 8 7 6 5 4 3 2 1

The paper used in this publication meets minimum requirements of the American National Standard for Information Sciences—Permanence of Paper for Printed Library Materials: ANSI Z39.48-1992.

Typeset in Minion

Composition by Oakland Street Publishing
Arlington, Virginia

Printed by R. R. Donnelley and Sons
Harrisonburg, Virginia

Contents

Preface

THE CONCLUSIONS OF THIS book are significantly at odds
with the assumptions I had when I started my research four years ago, in 1997.
In the best light, that observation is a testament to the objectivity of my
research. Less charitably, it may reflect only my lack of intuition at the outset.
In any case, my goal in launching the research that led to this work was to
quantify the potential benefits of humanitarian military intervention by examining what such intervention could have accomplished in the single worst
humanitarian atrocity of recent memory, the 1994 genocide in Rwanda. I
expected to confirm earlier claims that the international community—if it had
possessed sufficient political will—could have prevented the genocide with a
quick military intervention at minimal financial and human cost to the interveners. These findings, I assumed, would strengthen the case for such
interventions.

However, as they say, facts are stubborn things. Looking into the issue more
rigorously than my predecessors, I discovered that virtually all of the earlier
claims were inaccurate. The genocide happened much faster, the West learned
of it much later, and the requisite intervention would have been much slower
than previously claimed. Accordingly, I was compelled to reach a very differ-

ent conclusion: that a realistic intervention could not have prevented the genocide. Indeed, by my calculations, three-quarters of the Tutsi victims would
have died even if the West had launched a maximum intervention immediately upon learning that a nationwide genocide was being attempted in
Rwanda.

These unexpected findings compelled a new set of prescriptions. However,
contrary to some characterizations of my work, these prescriptions do not rule
out humanitarian intervention as a policy tool. Intervention does not have to
save every life in order to be worthwhile. In Rwanda, even if intervention
could have saved "only" one-quarter of the ultimate Tutsi victims, that still
means approximately 125,000 innocent lives could have been spared.

I also do not contend that the physical impediments to timely intervention—the speed of killing, the lack of accurate information, and the difficulty
of airlifting sufficient forces to Africa—are the sole reasons the international
community failed to intervene effectively during Rwanda's 1994 genocide.
Lack of political will also contributed, as evidenced by my finding that tens of
thousands of lives could have been saved by any of several realistic intervention options that were forgone. However, my study does refute the common
wisdom that merely a dearth of political will stood in the way of preventing
the genocide. Intervention advocates would do well to study these lessons.

In particular, two points stand out. First, if Western leaders are serious
about humanitarian military intervention, they can and should take several
concrete steps to improve its effectiveness. Second, and perhaps more important, intervention is no substitute for prevention. Rwanda and several other
recent cases demonstrate that massive ethnic violence can be inflicted faster
than the West can learn of it and deploy intervention forces to stop it. Thus if
the West relies mainly on military intervention to prevent genocide and ethnic cleansing, it is doomed to failure.

To stop such violence, the West must instead concentrate on averting its
outbreak in the first place. Because massive ethnic violence is most often the
consequence of escalating civil wars, this means the West should concentrate
most of its energies on de-escalating these conflicts. Sadly, current Western
policy often does just the opposite—offering rhetorical and military support for
armed secessionists and revolutionaries in the name of fighting oppression
and defending human rights, whether in Rwanda, Bosnia, Kosovo, East Timor,
Iraq, or elsewhere. As I have written earlier, while such Western support is well
intended, it often backfires by emboldening rebels to escalate their conflicts,
which in turn makes massive retaliation by government forces more likely.[1]
The Western reflex to support freedom fighters and condemn counterinsur-

gency campaigns is understandable, but statesmen should recognize that the unintended consequence of current policy may be to escalate civil wars and thereby increase the frequency and intensity of genocide and ethnic cleansing.

My hope is that this book will achieve two goals. First, it should promote debate about how to improve the efficacy of humanitarian military intervention, including how to confront some unavoidable trade-offs between improving mission effectiveness and reducing costs and risks to interveners. Second, by highlighting the inherent limitations of military options, the book should spur new focus on diplomacy toward ethnically divided societies. Such diplomacy confronts its own set of trade-offs, as it attempts to promote rapid improvement in the rights and welfare of disadvantaged groups without inadvertently raising hopes of impending intervention and thereby triggering an escalation of violence. The ultimate message of this book is that policymakers should be aware of the limitations—and possible unintended consequences—of military intervention when weighing that option against other alternatives. In some cases, military intervention still may be the right choice. That is why steps must be taken to optimize it.

For those of us who work on genocide and humanitarian intervention, the constant challenge is to transform "never again" from empty rhetoric into implementable policy. This book is intended in some small but positive way to contribute to that effort.

Acknowledgments

THIS BOOK WOULD NOT have been possible without the generous guidance, assistance, and support of many people and organizations. First and foremost, Professor Barry Posen of the Massachusetts Institute of Technology (MIT) provided invaluable insights into the analysis of military operations through his detailed critiques of several earlier drafts. Professor Filip Reyntjens of the University of Antwerp was an indispensable resource on Rwanda and the genocide. Alison Des Forges of Human Rights Watch provided generous advice during the early stages of my research. Many others provided valuable comments, including Professor Daryl Press of Dartmouth University, members of Harvard University's Belfer Center for Science and International Affairs, where I first presented my preliminary findings in December 1997, and four anonymous reviewers. Ultimately, I am solely responsible for the final manuscript and any errors of fact or interpretation that remain.

For financial support, I am indebted to MIT's Department of Political Science, the Institute for the Study of World Politics, the Brookings Institution, the Federation of American Scientists, the Harvard-MIT MacArthur Transnational Security program, the U.S. Institute of Peace, and Harvard University's

Belfer Center for Science and International Affairs. I also would like to thank Jim Hoge for publishing an excerpt of my research in the January–February 2000 issue of *Foreign Affairs*.

For her understanding, tolerance, support, and love over four years and through dozens of drafts of this manuscript, I will forever be grateful and indebted to Laila Al-Hamad. Finally, I dedicate this book to my mother, Carmel Kuperman, and my late father, Dr. Abraham S. Kuperman, who through love and example instilled in me a thirst for knowledge and the self-confidence to persevere to attain it.

THE LIMITS OF
HUMANITARIAN
INTERVENTION

CHAPTER ONE

The Common

Wisdom

SEVERAL YEARS AFTER mass killings of the 1990s in Bosnia, Somalia, and Rwanda, the United States still searches for a comprehensive policy to address deadly communal conflicts—those within a single territory pitting groups distinguished by ascriptive characteristics such as race, language, clan, caste, tribe, and religion. Among Washington policymakers and pundits, only two basic principles have achieved anything close to consensus. First, U.S. ground troops generally should not be deployed to humanitarian interventions in the midst of ongoing civil wars—a policy codified by the Clinton administration in 1994 as part of Presidential Decision Directive (PDD) 25 in the wake of U.S. soldiers' being killed in Somalia.[1] Second, an exception should be made to this general rule for cases of genocide, especially where intervention can succeed at low cost.

Support for intervention to stop genocide is voiced across the political spectrum. Conservative columnist Charles Krauthammer asks: "At what point does a violation of humanitarian norms become so extraordinary as to justify, indeed morally compel, military intervention? At the point of genocide. . . . [l]esser crimes have a claim on our sympathies but not our soldiers." A former Clinton administration official publicly urged her former boss in 1998 to

"state his readiness to use our own forces to halt genocide when the risk is pro-
portionally low and the probability of success high, as it was in Rwanda." On
the left, the human rights community likewise has urged that U.S. peacekeeping policy be "changed so that suppressing genocide was identified as a
vital American interest." Even former secretary of state Henry Kissinger has
stated that in the case of genocide, "the moral outrage has to predominate over
any considerations of power politics," and that in Rwanda he "personally
would have supported an intervention." President Bill Clinton concurred during his final year in office, declaring what some soon dubbed the Clinton
Doctrine: "If the world community has the power to stop it, we ought to stop
genocide and ethnic cleansing."[2] Even President George W. Bush, who stated
repeatedly during his presidential campaign that U.S. military troops should
not be deployed for purely humanitarian reasons, has said that the United
States should use its military assets to assist others who want to intervene in
genocidal situations such as Rwanda.[3]

Despite this amorphous belief among many foreign policy analysts that
the United States can and should do more when the next genocide arises,
there has been little hard thinking about just what that would entail and
what intervention could accomplish.[4] As a start, this book examines just
what a realistic U.S. military intervention could have accomplished in the last
indisputable case of genocide: Rwanda. In so doing, it tests the oft-repeated
claim that 5,000 troops deployed quickly could have averted the killing—and
finds it unsupportable. This claim originally was made by the UN's com-
manding general in Rwanda during the genocide and has since been
endorsed by members of Congress, human rights groups, and a distinguished panel of the Carnegie Commission on Preventing Deadly Conflict.
In reality, although some lives could have been saved by intervention at any
point during the genocide, even a large force deployed immediately upon
recognizing the genocidal intent would have arrived too late to save even half
of the ultimate victims.

Methodology and Counterfactuals

When analyzing what could have happened if government officials had
pursued a different policy, one enters the realm of what political scientists call
counterfactuals. Obviously, no hypothetical claim can ever be proved beyond
doubt. However, some counterfactual arguments are more convincing than
others. As James Fearon has argued, the two most important factors are *cotenability* and *legitimacy*.[5]

Cotenability requires that when analyzing the effects of a counterfactual premise one must also account for the effects of the other causal variables that could be affected by this premise. For example, if the premise is that a certain person had never been born, one must also account for the fact that this person's children and grandchildren would not have been born or done the things they did. Thus, in general, the broader the counterfactual assumption and the more distant in history from the consequences to be predicted, the less convincing is the argumentation—because to preserve cotenability, too many changes in too many variables, as well as the consequences of those changes, all would have to be predicted correctly. The most convincing counterfactual arguments, in terms of cotenability, are those in which the altered premise is narrow and would have occurred immediately before the predicted outcome.

The second factor, legitimacy, depends upon the plausibility of the counterfactual premise. If the premise is far-fetched, the counterfactual argument will not be compelling even if it observes cotenability. For example, one might argue that if the United States had not declared war against Japan in response to Japan's 1941 attack on Pearl Harbor, the Axis powers would have won World War II. However, because of the American public's fervent desire for revenge after Japan's attack, that premise is too implausible for the argument to be legitimate.

This study strives to satisfy both these criteria by restricting itself to a single counterfactual premise—that the president of the United States, upon determining that a genocide was in progress in Rwanda, had unilaterally ordered the expeditious deployment of a U.S. intervention force. Cotenability is facilitated by the premise's being narrow and the assumption that the deployment would have occurred immediately before the predicted consequences—that is, the number of lives saved by intervention. Legitimacy is preserved by the fact that this type of intervention to stop an ongoing genocide has been advocated by foreign-policy experts across the political spectrum, including President Clinton. By contrast, a less plausible premise would be that the United States had launched an intervention upon *initial* reports of violence, before any determination of genocide and without the permission of the Rwandan government. American foreign-policy experts generally do not support such uninvited U.S. military intervention into civil wars before having evidence of genocide because of the potential deleterious consequences: evisceration of the concept of sovereignty, proliferation of interventions, and dilution of U.S. military power.

This study avoids other counterfactual assumptions that have marred previous analyses—for example, that Washington officials could have known immediately upon the outbreak of violence in Rwanda that genocide was being attempted, that intervening forces could have arrived virtually overnight, and that U.S. military planners would have endangered servicemen by sending a force too small and poorly equipped to protect itself or to be confident of accomplishing the mission.[6] The hypothetical interventions discussed in this book assume only knowledge that was contemporaneously available or would have become so as a result of the intervention itself.

The preceding discussion is not intended to minimize the extent to which the book's single counterfactual assumption is in fact counterfactual, or to argue that early intervention would have been easy for U.S. officials to sell to the American public. It would have involved the unilateral deployment of U.S. forces to an ongoing civil conflict, in a distant country in which the United States has few historical ties, only six months after American deaths in Somalia soured Washington on such interventions and two weeks after the last American troops withdrew unilaterally from Somalia, in the face of ongoing U.S. commitments to a humanitarian airlift in Bosnia and the enforcement of no-fly zones in Bosnia and northern and southern Iraq, and likely before any UN authorization. Nevertheless, this choice of counterfactual assumption is appropriate for investigating rigorously the repeated claims by advocacy groups and the media that a small deployment of U.S. troops or some other military force could have prevented the Rwandan genocide. Considering that the U.S. military is without peer in force projection, and that coalition efforts generally are not synergistic, examining an all-American intervention can establish a benchmark for what any similarly sized force could have hoped to accomplish.

The assumption of a unilateral intervention without UN authorization is not unrealistic in the context of ongoing mass murder. When France ultimately launched its Operation Turquoise late during the Rwandan genocide, it deployed troops to Rwanda's border and announced they would enter with or without UN authorization, which was granted only on the eve of the troops' entry. Likewise, NATO's 1999 air campaign against Serbia, though a coalition effort, was a humanitarian military intervention launched without UN authorization. If in April 1994 the president of the United States had announced his determination to intervene in Rwanda to stop genocide, it would have been hard for anyone to argue credibly for delaying the intervention to obtain UN authorization or to form a multilateral coalition while thousands of civilians were being slaughtered daily.

CHAPTER TWO

Roots of the
Rwandan Tragedy

BEFORE AND DURING the colonial period, Rwanda was dominated politically by Tutsi, a social group comprising 17 percent of the population. Virtually all the rest of the population was Hutu. Less than 1 percent were aboriginal Twa. All three groups lived intermingled in Rwanda for hundreds of years. Although the Tutsi have a separate heritage and apparently entered the region somewhat later than the Hutu, the term "tribe" or "ethnic group" has long been inappropriate to distinguish between these two main Rwandan groups. They share a common language and religions, and have intermarried. In recent decades, however, the Hutu-Tutsi distinction has become very salient owing to several factors: the struggle for political power in Rwanda, physical insecurity during periods of civil war, a Tutsi refugee crisis, and certain self-policed restrictions on intermarriage.[1]

Historians divide into two camps regarding the nature of Hutu-Tutsi relations before European colonization.[2] One view, endorsed by Tutsi politicians and espoused by many Western historians, including Gérard Prunier, contends that relations between the two groups generally were symbiotic rather than antagonistic until the arrival of colonial powers in the late nineteenth century. This school does not dispute that Tutsi kings ruled over most of Rwanda during the precolonial period, but contends that many administrators had been Hutu and that patron-client relationships between and within each group were flexible and mutually beneficial. Tutsi tended to be cattle owners, and Hutu were usually cultivators, but these distinctions were not rigid.

This school argues that it was first Germany and—after the transfer of colonial authority during World War I—Belgium that sharpened ethnic distinctions in Rwanda to implement a system of indirect rule. Neither European power deployed a large number of its citizens to colonize or administer Rwanda, so they were forced to appoint local officials to oversee the extraction of resources. Because Tutsi dominated the precolonial royalty and were viewed by European ethnographers of the time as superior to the rest of the populace, they were selected to head the local administration. By this reading of history, it was European demands for resource extraction that bastardized Rwanda's social system, forced a small group of Tutsi administrators to oppress the Hutu majority, and thereby polarized and hardened ethnic identities.

Hutu politicians and other historians disagree, contending that Tutsi rule even before the arrival of the Europeans imposed a discriminatory two-tier system. This school holds that the colonial powers merely formalized and institutionalized a pre-existing racist system by taking steps such as issuing identity cards that listed group affiliation. Thus there is substantial disagreement as to whether the precolonial Hutu-Tutsi relationship was one of symbiosis or domination. However, both schools agree that during the colonial period an elite group of Tutsi exploited Hutu as second-class citizens.

In the mid-1950s, the Tutsi began to embrace ideas of decolonization that were spreading across Africa. Belgium had begun to switch its allegiance toward the majority Hutu, which spurred the Tutsi to push even harder to obtain independence while they still retained political dominance. In their quest, the Tutsi obtained support from international communist sources, which only reinforced Belgium's shift. Meanwhile the Hutu were building their own political movement based on the historical claim that the Tutsi had subjugated the Hutu for hundreds of years. They mobilized around the platform that Rwanda was a Hutu nation that had to throw off the yoke of centuries of Tutsi oppression, calling their movement the Parti du Mouvement et de l'Emancipation des Bahutu (PARMEHUTU), or Hutu Emancipation Party. Thus the Hutu independence movement was based even more on liberation from internal Tutsi domination than from external colonial authority.

Large-scale violence between Rwanda's Hutu and Tutsi erupted for the first time in 1959, as the Hutu mobilized their masses to seize power. Belgium deployed troops who temporarily quelled violence and facilitated the transfer of political power to the Hutu. The Hutu consolidated this new power in a 1961 referendum, but only after burning houses, killing hundreds of Tutsi, and triggering the flight of tens of thousands more to neighboring countries—mainly Uganda, Burundi, Tanzania, and Zaire. Formal independence was granted to the Hutu regime of President Grégoire Kayibanda on July 1, 1962.

Starting in 1961, however, a group of Tutsi refugees attempted to return to power in Rwanda by launching attacks from bases in Uganda and Burundi. These Tutsi rebels were known as the "*inyenzi*," or cockroaches, for their propensity to return repeatedly at night despite attempts to stamp them out. Although eventually the term became one of derision when employed by Hutu, it apparently was adopted originally by the rebels themselves as a symbol of their relentlessness.

In response to these repeated attacks by Tutsi refugee rebels in the 1960s, Rwanda's hard-line Hutu nationalist government escalated its oppression of and attacks against Tutsi within the country. The government's policy was intended to reduce domestic support for the rebels and to deter any further attacks, and it caused many more Tutsi to flee as refugees. The most successful of the inyenzi attacks occurred in 1963—when Tutsi from Burundi came within ten miles of the Rwandan capital, Kigali—but this also triggered the most intense outburst of reprisal killing against Tutsi. Ultimately, the government's tactics, though horrific, proved effective in reducing the incidence of inyenzi attacks, which ended in 1967. Overall, from 1959 to 1967, some 20,000 Tutsi were killed. Another 200,000 Tutsi—half their population in Rwanda at the time—were driven from the country as refugees, not to return for at least two decades. As a result, the Tutsi percentage of Rwanda's population dropped from about 17 to 9 percent, with Hutu representing virtually all the rest.[3]

After the end of the inyenzi invasions, the remaining Tutsi population of Rwanda was spared further significant outbursts of violence until the waning days of the PARMEHUTU regime in 1973. In that year President Kayibanda faced mounting internal criticism for his ineffective rule and favoritism toward his home region of south-central Rwanda, so he attempted to revive pan-Hutu support for his regime by blaming Rwanda's remaining Tutsi for the country's ills and renewing attacks against them. However, this strategy was short-lived because Kayibanda was overthrown in July 1973 by a Hutu army officer from northwestern Rwanda, Juvénal Habyarimana.

As the new president, Habyarimana declared that he would put an end to ethnic violence in Rwanda and lived up to this promise for the next seventeen years. Discrimination in Rwanda during this period was not anti-Tutsi, but rather in favor of a narrow section of the Hutu population who came from the president's home region in northwestern Rwanda. This favored regional group dominated key positions in government, business, the army, and Habyarimana's single ruling party, the Mouvement Révolutionnaire National pour le Développement (MRND). In addition, the northwest region received the lion's share of government investment. The rest of the country, both Hutu and Tutsi, suffered from relative neglect. On the whole, however, Rwanda thrived for the first fifteen years of Habyarimana's regime, benefiting from political stability, ample commodity prices, and foreign development assistance to achieve by far the best economic growth of any state in east-central Africa during this period.[4]

Habyarimana's handling of the Tutsi question was complex. On the one hand, he ensured that there were no further violent attacks against Tutsi for the first seventeen years of his rule and permitted some Tutsi to become prominent businessmen and even personal friends. However, he prohibited Tutsi refugees from returning to Rwanda. He also subjected domestic Tutsi to quotas for access to government-controlled programs such as education, limiting them to their percentage of the population in what Americans might call an "affirmative action" program to compensate Hutu for historical discrimination. In sum, Habyarimana was willing to protect Rwanda's small Tutsi population and to benefit from Tutsi business activities, but he felt it necessary to block the return of refugees and perpetuate quotas in order to prevent the Tutsi from developing a power center that could challenge his authority.

In the late 1980s, however, Habyarimana's authority began to be challenged by several other developments. First, declining global agricultural prices undermined Rwanda's economy, which depended heavily on tea exports. This spurred increasing domestic political opposition, especially from the neglected south-central region of the country that had been the base of the PARMEHUTU. Second, the international community started to pressure Habyarimana to democratize and to resolve the long-standing Tutsi refugee issue, which had contributed to instability in some of the host countries for thirty years. Third, Habyarimana was aware that Uganda's army contained many Rwandan Tutsi refugees, who were rumored to be considering an armed invasion of Rwanda. In an attempt to head off these challenges, Habyarimana in 1990 initiated a series of reforms—albeit mainly superficial—toward democratization and refugee return. However, before the sincerity of the reforms could be put to the test, the armed Tutsi refugees invaded from Uganda on October 1, 1990, under the banner of a party called the Rwandan Patriotic Front (RPF) and its military wing, the Rwandan Patriotic Army (RPA).

The Tutsi leaders of the RPF originally had fought for Ugandan rebel Yoweri Museveni in the 1970s and 1980s in that country's civil wars, first against President Idi Amin and then to overthrow President Milton Obote successfully in 1986. After helping to bring Museveni to power in Kampala in 1986, many top Tutsi rebels became senior officials in Uganda's army, where they helped recruit thousands more Tutsi refugees to become soldiers. As the Tutsi thereby gained access to arms and military training but continued to face ethnic hostility from many Ugandans, it was perhaps inevitable that the Tutsi soldiers would defect and invade back into Rwanda, despite Habyarimana's nascent reforms.

Although Habyarimana previously had been a protector of the Tutsi who lived within Rwanda, he reacted to the invasion much as his extremist predecessor had done decades earlier, by arresting politically active Tutsi in the capital, Kigali, and permitting intermittent massacres against Tutsi in the countryside. In addition, France, Belgium, and Zaire intervened immediately in support of the government's efforts to combat the rebels. France deployed 350 troops, and Zaire deployed 500 of its elite Presidential Guard on behalf of the government; Belgium deployed 540 troops to Kigali's airport in preparation for a possible evacuation of foreign nationals. Benefiting from this foreign support, the Rwandan army quickly beat back the rebels, who initially were ill-organized and ill-equipped because they had defected from disparate Ugandan army units immediately before the invasion. After the rebels retreated into the mountains on the Ugandan border, Belgium withdrew its troops and Habyarimana asked Zaire to withdraw its troops because they were accused of pillaging. However, France maintained its military deployment on behalf of Habyarimana's government for several more years. This fit with France's general policy at the time of absorbing Belgium's sphere of influence in central Africa in order to maintain the region's francophone quality, as Belgium withdrew from the continent in response to increasing ethical and financial concerns about the postcolonial role.[5]

Although Habyarimana was able to rely temporarily on French military backing to prevent his overthrow, the French also insisted that he pursue a transition to multiparty democracy. The French government made clear to Habyarimana that its military support could not last forever and that he had to broaden his domestic support and legitimacy to survive the transition to democracy. Habyarimana responded with grudging concessions toward pluralization in 1991 and 1992, although without ever actually devolving real power. Other Western states then applied even stronger coercive pressure, threatening to suspend aid and trade—and in some cases doing so—to force Habyarimana to commit to reforms and to honor those commitments.

The Tutsi rebels, for their part, regrouped within months of their initial defeat. By 1991 they held a small swath of territory in the north and had forced Habyarimana to the negotiating table to arrange a cease-fire. As the rebels progressed militarily, they also forged uneasy political alliances with the opposition parties then emerging in Rwanda. On the surface, some of these alliances were quite bizarre. For example, the RPF, an organization of Tutsi refugees, was cooperating with the Mouvement Démocratique Républicain (MDR), which was the reincarnation of the Hutu nationalist PARMEHUTU that had ethnically cleansed the Tutsi from Rwanda in the first place. But the two parties needed each other. The MDR could not get Habyarimana to negotiate seriously without the military pressure applied by the Tutsi rebels. And the RPF, whose natural constituency consisted only of the minority Tutsi refugee community, could not gain political legitimacy in Rwanda and internationally unless it was seen working with the Hutu majority. Thus the temporary alliance suited both sides.

Another successful rebel offensive in 1992 again forced Habyarimana to the negotiating table—this time comprehensive, internationally supervised peace talks in the town of Arusha, Tanzania. After making progress on matters such as refugee return, the talks bogged down over two crucial issues of power-sharing: Which parties would be represented in a transitional government before elections? And how would the rebel and government troops be integrated into a combined army? Habyarimana and his Hutu cronies from northwestern Rwanda feared that, if the Tutsi rebels and their allies within the Rwandan opposition were allowed to dominate the transition government and army, the outcome would amount to a negotiated coup. Under this scenario, the Hutu elite feared they would at best lose the privileges of rule, and at worst suffer deadly retribution for their years of corruption and favoritism.

In early 1993, with the negotiations stalled, Rwandan Hutu extremists perpetrated another of their periodic massacres of Tutsi, which had started in response to the 1990 invasion. This attack raised the toll of Tutsi victims to about 2,000 during the preceding two and a half years. In retaliation, the RPF launched yet another offensive. Fortified by three years of training and battlefield experience, the rebels had become a formidable force and they advanced rapidly toward the capital, appearing poised to capture it. But France then deployed another 240 troops, who joined 250 troops still there—an infusion of support that bolstered the confidence and performance of the Rwandan army and deterred the rebels from further advances. Although this

French force was too small to enable a Rwandan army victory on the battle-field, the rebels nevertheless agreed to a cease-fire because they feared that pressing the fight would prompt France to send more reinforcements and could cost them the hard-won diplomatic support of the international community by making them appear too militant.[6]

Habyarimana, however, began to feel increasing pressure from all sides—military pressure from the rebels, political pressure from domestic Hutu, and economic pressure from Western powers—exacerbated by France's insistence that it soon would be removing its troops, which he correctly saw as his only protection against the rebels. In August 1993, seeing little other choice, he finally caved in on the two power-sharing provisions and signed the comprehensive Arusha accords. The RPF and the domestic opposition were to be given the majority of seats in the interim cabinet and legislature before elections. Moreover, the rebels were to be granted 50 percent of the officer positions (and 40 percent of the enlisted ranks) in the combined army. In light of the superiority of the rebels on a man-for-man basis by this time, the military integration protocol was tantamount to a negotiated surrender of the Hutu army to the Tutsi rebels.

Habyarimana's cronies felt betrayed and terrified. They immediately set out to undermine the implementation of the accords, working in conjunction with Habyarimana. UN peacekeepers arrived in late 1993 to replace French forces, as called for in the accords, but this switch only exacerbated the paranoia of the governing Hutu elite, which felt it was losing its last line of defense. Ironically, while the French have been widely blamed for contributing to the genocide by supporting the Hutu government of Habyarimana, it was actually this French military *withdrawal* that raised Hutu fears to the breaking point and prompted the final radicalization of politics that culminated in the genocide.

Habyarimana obstructed and attempted to modify the implementation of the accords for eight months. He hoped to retain power by splitting the alliance of convenience that had formed between the Tutsi rebels and the domestic Hutu opposition by convincing the latter to support him in a pan-Hutu alliance against the Tutsi. Ironically, Habyarimana was helped in this effort by the February 1993 Tutsi rebel offensive, which had proved to be a tactical military success but a strategic disaster. The rebels, by advancing so close to the capital, had renewed fears among Rwanda's Hutu that the RPF's real goal was to conquer Rwanda exclusively for the Tutsi. Moderate Hutu in Rwanda's opposition political parties began to suspect they were being used as stalking horses by the Tutsi, to be discarded after the rebels took power through force or negotiation. These fears were further stoked in October 1993, when Tutsi in neighboring Burundi assassinated that country's first Hutu president and killed thousands of Hutu civilians.

As ethnic fear increased, Habyarimana employed a combination of bribery and populist appeals to pan-Hutu solidarity to successfully convince the dominant factions in all but one of the main opposition parties to break with the rebels. By doing so, he effectively split each of these opposition parties in two—a pro-rebel faction and a more powerful pan-Hutu (or "Hutu Power") faction.[7] As a result, it became impossible to implement the transitional government called for in the Arusha accords because each of the parties submitted two competing names for each seat in the transitional government that it was assigned by the Arusha framework. Further complicating matters, Habyarimana insisted that this framework be modified to add an extreme Hutu nationalist party to the government, the Coalition pour la Défense de la République (CDR), which the RPF refused to consider. So long as the transition government could not be implemented, however, Habyarimana retained power.[8] The Tutsi rebels, growing increasingly frustrated with these delays, prepared for a possible final military offensive to conquer the country.

At the same time, extreme elements within the ruling Hutu clique prepared their own "final solution" to retain power and block what they perceived as a Tutsi attempt to reconquer Rwanda after thirty-five years of Hutu emancipation. These Hutu extremists apparently believed that by preparing to kill all of the Tutsi civilians in Rwanda they could prevent the country from being conquered by the rebels. Accordingly, they imported thousands of guns and grenades and hundreds of thousands of machetes. They also converted and expanded existing political party youth wings, which previously had engaged only in low-level physical intimidation, into fully fledged armed militias and provided some of them with formal military training. To foment Hutu fear and anti-Tutsi hatred they also created a new private radio station as an alternative to the existing government channel. Apparently they also established a clandestine network of extremists within the army to take charge when the time came. As the Tutsi rebels picked up indications of this activity in early 1994, they began training in earnest for the resumption of war, which only further fed Hutu fears. This crescendo of fear was further propelled in February 1994 by a wave of mutual political assassinations.

Finally, on April 6, 1994, as President Habyarimana was flying back to Rwanda from a conference in Tanzania, he was killed when his private plane was shot down by surface-to-air missiles on approach to Kigali. Hutu extremists quickly blamed the Tutsi rebels for the attack and seized effective control of the government. Within hours, they commenced the genocide of Tutsi, as well as an assassination campaign against all moderate opposition politicians, whether Hutu or Tutsi. In two days the extremists had wiped out the opposition and established a new "interim" government that would oversee the killing of Tutsi. It still remains unclear who shot down the plane and why. It is possible that the extremist Hutu launched the attack because Habyarimana was perceived to be succumbing to Western pressure to implement the Arusha accords, and his assassination also provided a pretext for a genocide to which they were already committed. However, it also is possible that the Tutsi rebels had grown frustrated with Habyarimana's refusal to implement the Arusha accords and fearful that a genocide might be imminent, so they decided to assassinate the president and resume the war in the expectation of a quick victory. If the latter scenario is correct, it would call into question whether the genocide was planned by the extremist Hutu as a proactive initiative or was merely a contingency plan. It also remains unclear whether the genocide was intended from the start to continue until total annihilation of the Tutsi, or whether the Hutu extremists might have been willing to suspend it in return for rebel agreement to a cease-fire and renegotiation of the Arusha accords. What is more clear are the facts of the genocide, to which we now turn.

CHAPTER THREE

Mechanics of
the Genocide

THE GENOCIDE HAS BEEN documented best in two large volumes by human rights organizations. Immediately after the genocide, African Rights compiled the testimony of survivors.[1] More recently, Human Rights Watch produced a history that explores how the genocide's leaders implemented their plan, especially in those areas where local political authorities initially opposed the killing.[2] Both accounts report a chilling regularity to the progression of genocide.

The following description of the genocide's progression was constructed from accounts in the African Rights volume. The book, based on survivors' testimony, does not purport to be a scientific survey and has at least one obvious selection bias in that it cannot report massacres in which everyone was killed, since no survivors could give their testimony. However, the book's authors attempted to document as much of the genocide as possible. The authenticity of their documentation of the genocide has not been questioned, aside from the contention by Des Forges that death totals at some sites are inflated and specific dates may be off by a day or two.[3] Most important, there is no reason to suspect an intentional or accidental bias related to timing, unless the unavoidable selection bias already mentioned is correlated with time. Thus when the book reports that all or a vast majority of the massacre-related

deaths in one prefecture occurred before a particular date, it appears reasonable to conclude that a majority of the genocide there was carried out by
approximately that date. Conversely, when all or a vast majority of the massacre-related deaths in another prefecture are reported to have occurred after
a particular date, it appears reasonable to conclude that most Tutsi were still
alive before that date. Providing additional confirmation, Human Rights
Watch reports a similar geographic progression of the genocide.

In most areas of Rwanda, violence began on April 7, 1994, the day after the
president's plane was shot down. Government Radio Rwanda and the extremists' Radio-Television Libre des Mille Collines (RTLM) urged Hutu to take
vengeance against Tutsi for their alleged murder of the president. Led by militias, Hutu began to attack the homes of neighboring Tutsi, attempting to rob,
rape, and murder them, often setting fire to their homes. This initial step did
not cause the death of a high proportion of Tutsi because Hutu were usually
poorly armed. Rather, the vast majority of Tutsi fled their homes and sought
refuge in the central gathering places of their communes—churches, schools,
hospitals, athletic fields, stadiums, and other accessible spaces.[4] It was common
for Tutsi to pass through more than one such site, progressively aggregating in
larger concentrations voluntarily or at government direction. Within a few
days, most of Rwanda's more than half-million Tutsi were congregated at sites
throughout the country, in groups typically ranging from a few hundred to
tens of thousands.

At first, this strategy gave the Tutsi a defensive advantage. The surrounding
crowds of militia-led Hutu generally were armed only with knives of various
sorts—swords, spears, machetes—or the traditional *masu*, a large club stud-
ded with nails.[5] The assembled Tutsi, whose primary weapons were rocks,
often were able to deter or fend off attacks and use existing structures for
defense. By contrast, individual Tutsi who attempted to flee were typically
killed immediately by the surrounding masses or were caught and killed at
roadblocks. For several days, this produced a stand-off. Tutsi living conditions
were deteriorating and supplies dwindling, but the Hutu generally were
unwilling to risk casualties by attacking.

In most parts of Rwanda this situation changed by about April 13, one week
into the violence, when better-armed Hutu reinforcements—composed
of regular army, reservists, the Presidential Guard, or national police
(*gendarmerie*)—began arriving at the Tutsi gathering sites.[6] Though these
forces were few in number at each site, they were armed with rifles, grenades,
and machine guns, which tilted the balance of forces. Typically, a few grenades
would be tossed in on the Tutsi, followed by light arms fire.[7] Those Tutsi not

killed or wounded by the initial fusillade often attempted to flee, whereupon they usually were cut down by gunfire or surrounded and killed by the mob. Militia-led Hutu then would enter the site and hack to death those still alive. Some Tutsi escaped in the initial mayhem or avoided death by lying still beneath their dead compatriots. However, many were later caught at road-blocks and killed on the spot or taken to other central sites to face the entire ordeal again. A few lucky Tutsi survived by hiding in places such as pit latrines or the ceilings of homes of sympathetic Hutu, living to tell their harrowing tales.

Perhaps the most remarkable and least appreciated aspect of the genocide was its speed. Based on the testimonies reported by African Rights, the majority of Tutsi gathering sites were attacked and destroyed before April 21, only fifteen days into the genocide. Given that half or more of the Tutsi victims died at central gathering sites,[8] the unavoidable conclusion is that a large portion of Rwanda's Tutsi were killed by April 21—perhaps 250,000 in just over two weeks.[9] That rate of killing would make it the fastest genocide in recorded history.

Despite this pattern, the fates of another several hundred thousand Tutsi were different for two main reasons. First was the presence of foreigners. Hutu extremists generally avoided perpetrating large-scale massacres when international observers were present, as part of a comprehensive strategy to hide the genocide from both the outside world and Rwanda's Tutsi until it could be completed. Also part of this strategy, the Hutu severed virtually all telephone links between Kigali and the countryside during the first week of the genocide, by about April 12 or 13, 1994, although lines within Kigali and international lines to Kigali functioned intermittently during the genocide. To orchestrate the genocide, the government maintained other lines of com-munication to civil administrators, including military transmissions and the radio.[10]

Where Tutsi were congregated under the watch of outside observers, the extremists pursued an alternative strategy of slow, stealthy annihilation. Typ-ically, Hutu leaders arrived each day at such sites with a list of up to several dozen names, usually starting with the Tutsi political elite. These Tutsi were removed under a false pretense such as interrogation, then taken to a remote location and executed. This occurred at several sites across Rwanda: Kama-rampaka Stadium and Nyarushishi camp in Cyangugu prefecture, where International Committee of the Red Cross (ICRC) aid workers were present; the Kabgayi Archbishopric in Gitarama prefecture, under the watchful eye of the Pope's top representatives; Amahoro stadium in Kigali city, where United Nations Assistance Mission for Rwanda (UNAMIR) troops stood guard; as well as smaller sites in Kigali City such as St. Famille and St. Paul's churches.[11]

At such sites, the vast majority of Tutsi were still alive at the end of April, and a good number survived the entire ordeal.

Thus, interestingly, it appears that the modest deterrent impact of UNAMIR troops may have been more a function of their being foreign than their being armed, considering that the unarmed ICRC had a similar deterrent impact. Another factor that spared Tutsi at the Cyangugu sites was the presence of a national-police official opposed to the killing. At Kabgayi, top church officials with direct ties to Rome attempted to and did deter large-scale killing on their site. However, most lower-level indigenous religious officials throughout Rwanda were not able to deter the genocide or cooperated with its perpetrators.[12]

The second and more important cause of variation in the fate of the Tutsi was regional differences in the politics and history of Rwanda's traditional ten prefectures.[13] Byumba prefecture, bordering Uganda in the north, already was partially controlled by the Tutsi-led rebels when the president's plane was shot down, and they quickly occupied the rest, so massacres of Tutsi were largely avoided there. The two prefectures most dominated by Hutu extremists, Gisenyi and Ruhengeri in the northwest, ironically also suffered relatively little killing because much of their Tutsi populations had fled before the genocide in response to earlier threats and harassment.

Two prefectures with high Tutsi populations and strong Hutu opposition movements also managed initially to avoid the genocide. Butare prefecture, in the south, was governed by a Tutsi prefect who managed to prevent militias from entering the prefecture until he was removed from office on April 18. Widespread killing then commenced with a vengeance, as tens of thousands of Tutsi perished in the first few days.[14] Gitarama prefecture in central Rwanda was the heart of majority Hutu opposition to the regime dominated by Hutu from northwestern Rwanda, and thus likewise resisted implementing the genocide until government forces arrived to spur them. Indeed, in Gitarama, even the extremist Hutu Power wing of the opposition MDR party initially opposed the genocide, which it perceived correctly as linked to a power grab by the ruling party and the allied CDR party. In short order, however, after the resumption of civil war against the Tutsi-led Rwandan Patriotic Front, such intra-Hutu conflict quickly was put aside, as the extremists intended all along. Large-scale killing commenced in Gitarama about April 21.[15]

By late April, only three weeks after the president's assassination, almost all the large massacres were finished (see figure 3-1). The rebels themselves acknowledged on April 29 that "the genocide is almost completed." This conclusion was reiterated the following day by the RPF political bureau. Soon after, on May 11, rebel radio declared, "The genocide is already finished."[16] It

Figure 3-1. *Geographic Progression of the Genocide from April 7, 1994*

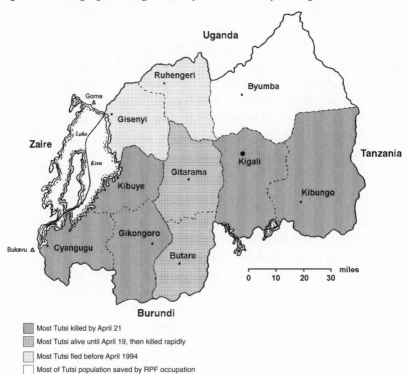

Most Tutsi killed by April 21

Most Tutsi alive until April 19, then killed rapidly

Most Tutsi fled before April 1994

Most of Tutsi population saved by RPF occupation

appears the rebels did believe that most Tutsi already had been killed. How-ever, the RPF also had a strategic motivation for announcing this conclusion at such an early date—to justify its opposition to renewed UN military inter-vention that it feared could interfere with a military victory by the RPF.

Human Rights Watch concurs that "in general, the worst massacres had finished by the end of April." By that time, "perhaps half of the Tutsi popu-lation of Rwanda"—some two-thirds of the ultimate Tutsi victims—already had been exterminated.[17] Subsequently, Tutsi who had avoided the initial massacres continued to be killed gradually at roadblocks or by roving bands of armed Hutu. As the RPF captured territory, the killing of Tutsi generally declined in rebel-occupied zones, but sometimes persisted in outlying areas of these zones for several days because the rebels lacked sufficient troops to blanket the countryside.[18]

The pattern of killing in Kigali city also differed significantly from that in the rest of the country. During the first two days the extremist Hutu worked from prepared lists to perpetrate a highly organized and thorough assassination campaign, starting with opposition politicians and moving to prominent liberals such as human rights advocates. Ironically, these first victims of violence by the extremist Hutu organizers and perpetrators of the genocide were mainly fellow Hutu—moderates and those who had allied themselves with the Tutsi rebels.[19]

On the first full day of killing, April 7, the rebels mobilized their forces in the north, and an RPA battalion that had been stationed in Kigali since December 1993 under the Arusha accords issued an ultimatum for violence to end. When it did not, the battalion engaged government forces, igniting civil war in the capital.[20] With the president and moderate opposition dead, civil war breaking out in Kigali for the first time, and radio broadcasts urging Hutu to kill their neighbors, the capital descended into chaos. Corpses began to pile up in Kigali, totaling as many as 20,000 during the first week. Contrary to the situation in the countryside, however, Tutsi able to flee to central gathering sites in Kigali gained a degree of refuge owing to the heavier presence of foreigners. The extremists could not hide the chaos and violence, but they tried to avoid wholesale massacres in front of outside witnesses.

Precise Tutsi death totals are difficult to determine because of several factors, including the inability to distinguish Tutsi from Hutu corpses. Estimates can be made by subtracting the number of Tutsi survivors from the number living in Rwanda immediately before the genocide. However, even the pregenocide population is disputed. In 1991 the government of Rwanda conducted a comprehensive census, reporting that 8.27 percent of Rwandans were Tutsi. Some scholars suspect an undercount for at least two reasons. First, the Hutu government had incentive to lower the percentage because it served as the basis for Tutsi entitlements under Rwanda's quota system. Second, some Tutsi undoubtedly succeeded in "passing" as Hutu to escape the quotas.[21]

However, historical demographic evidence suggests the census figures are fairly accurate, and there is no justification for Gérard Prunier's sharp upward adjustment of the pregenocide Tutsi figure to 12 percent. In 1956, Belgium's final colonial census reported Tutsi as 16.59 percent of Rwanda's population.[22] If this percentage had any bias, one would expect it to be upward, because Hutu had incentive at the time to try to pass as the more favored Tutsi. Thus, of Rwanda's total 1959 population of approximately 2.6 million, there were no more than about 430,000 Tutsi. In the several years of tumult surrounding independence, an estimated 20,000 Tutsi were killed and approximately 200,000 fled as refugees.[23] These events reduced the number of Tutsi in Rwanda by approximately half, to about 9 percent of the remaining population in 1965.

Supporting this conclusion, a 1978 census reported Tutsi as 9.64 percent of the population. Tutsi also had a lower reported fertility rate than Hutu in postindependence Rwanda, so the Tutsi proportion should have declined gradually over time. Other migration of Hutu and Tutsi into and out of Rwanda from 1965 to 1994 was not large enough to significantly alter these proportions.

In this light, the 8.27 percent figure reported by the Rwandan government in the 1991 census appears credible, whereas Prunier's higher estimate does not. The lower figure also is supported by Human Rights Watch, which states that there is no evidence the Rwandan government manipulated the census figures. Some Tutsi undoubtedly passed as Hutu, but the numbers were small.[24] Thus this book relies on the 1991 census, acknowledging that it represents a conservative (low-end) estimate of the percentage of Tutsi. Estimated 1994 population figures are extrapolated from the census based on the country's rapid annual 3 percent growth rate.

These assumptions suggest that Rwanda's pregenocide population included approximately 650,000 Tutsi. After the genocide and civil war, some 150,000 Tutsi survivors were identified by aid organizations.[25] Thus an estimated 500,000 Rwandan Tutsi were killed, or more than three-quarters of their population in the country. Human Rights Watch concurs with these estimates. It may never be possible to determine more precisely how many Tutsi were killed, in part because of definitional issues. For example, if a Rwandan's identity card said he was a Hutu, but the militias killed him because they suspected he was really a Tutsi, it is not clear how the victim should be categorized.[26]

The number of Hutu killed during the genocide and civil war is even less certain, with estimates ranging from 10,000 to well over 100,000. Gérard Prunier estimates that 10,000 to 30,000 Hutu moderates were killed during the genocide by Hutu extremists. In addition, the Tutsi-led rebels killed an estimated 60,000 Hutu from April 1994 through August 1995, according to Seth Sendashonga, a former Hutu member of the RPF who later was assassinated. Extrapolating from documented incidents, Filip Reyntjens estimates that the RPF actually killed even more Hutu over a shorter period—some 100,000 from April 1994 to October 1994. RPF atrocities against Hutu were first alleged by the United Nations High Commissioner for Refugees (UNHCR) barely one month into the anti-Tutsi genocide in mid-May 1994 and were formally compiled in a September 1994 UNHCR report by Robert Gersony that still had not been released in early 2001. In addition to political killings of Hutu by Hutu extremists and the Tutsi-led rebels, Reyntjens notes that many Hutu were killed by fellow Hutu in sheer criminal violence. However, none of these estimates accounts for the total number of Hutu missing after the genocide.

Figure 3-2. *Estimated Quantitative Progression of the Genocide from April 7, 1994*

Surviving Tutsi

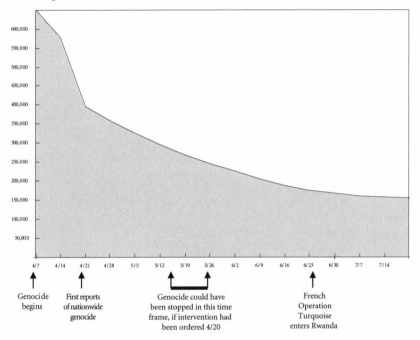

Statistics comparing Rwandan population figures before and after the genocide indicate that 1.1 million Rwandans appear to have died or gone missing between April 1994 and Spring 1995. Reyntjens estimates that no more than 600,000 of those victims could have been Tutsi, and that perhaps 50,000 Hutu died of illness in the refugee camps. If he is correct, several hundred thousand Hutu deaths or disappearances remain unexplained. One possibility is that the killing of Hutu by the RPF in reprisal was even greater than estimated; a second is that many Hutu were mistaken for Tutsi and killed by other Hutu as part of the genocide; a third is that many Hutu were missed by census counts after the genocide.[27]

A model has been constructed to estimate the quantitative progression of the anti-Tutsi genocide over time, based on its geographic progression and the prefecture-level population data in the 1991 census. The model does not purport to be a precise record of the killing, which would require comprehensive data that may never be available. Rather, it is intended to offer insight into the rate of killing over time and the potential for various types of intervention to have saved lives. The model's assumptions are contained in Appendix A and its conclusions depicted graphically in figure 3-2.

CHAPTER FOUR

When Did
We Know?

AMERICAN INTELLIGENCE REPORTS from the period of the genocide remain classified. U.S. officials who had responsibility for Rwanda, however, assert that classified reports from the first few weeks of violence largely mirrored open reporting at the time by international news media, human rights organizations, and the United Nations.[1] Indeed, these officials say they relied heavily on such open reporting rather than on proprietary U.S. government sources of information.[2] In part, this was because the normal sources of proprietary intelligence were not available in Rwanda. Soon after the outbreak of violence, American embassy personnel were restricted to their homes until evacuation and so could not engage in normal intelligence gathering. In addition, because the region was considered a low priority, the United States maintained only a single human intelligence asset in central Africa before the genocide—a defense attaché in Cameroon—who was responsible for covering at least two other countries in addition to Rwanda.[3] Nevertheless, during the first few days of violence, Washington officials did manage to communicate with other contacts in Rwanda, including UN peacekeepers, French and Belgian evacuation troops, human rights workers, and opposition Tutsi and moderate Hutu politicians.[4] However, because these same sources also informed the open reporting by nongovernmental organizations (NGOs), they did not provide a distinct channel of classified intelligence.

Only one U.S. government organization, the Defense Intelligence Agency (DIA), appears to have had unique sources of information that permitted it to comprehend the progression of events somewhat sooner and more accurately than other government agencies or nongovernmental organizations. For a variety of reasons explored at the end of this chapter, however, such proprietary intelligence was not incorporated or utilized by other parts of the U.S. national security establishment—at the State Department, Central Intelligence Agency, National Security Council, or even other offices in the Pentagon—and so was not conveyed to President Clinton in processed intelligence reports. Thus, the best indication of what senior U.S. officials believed at the time and reported to the president in classified intelligence reports is the concurrent open reporting by the media, UN, and human rights organizations.

To document the progression of this open-source intelligence on the genocide as it was occurring, I conducted a review of international reporting by American, British, French, Belgian, and Rwandan media, leading human rights groups, and UN officials. This review includes the following: all daily editions of *The Times*, *The Guardian*, and *Le Monde* from April 6 to April 30, 1994; results of a Lexis/Nexis search of all stories about Rwanda in the *Washington Post* and *New York Times* from April 6 to May 14, 1994; and all reports in the CIA's Foreign Broadcast Information Service (FBIS) for Africa and Western Europe from April 6 to April 30, 1994, which includes radio and newspaper reports from Rwanda (both rebel and government sources), Belgium, Britain, and France. Although some observers consider U.S. newspapers to be notoriously inaccurate or belated sources of information about Africa, I included two leading American newspapers in this review to indicate how and when the American public and much of official Washington learned of the genocide.

This comprehensive review suggests strongly that, because of five trends in the reporting during the first two weeks, the president of the United States could not have determined that a nationwide genocide was under way in Rwanda until about April 20, 1994. First, violence was initially depicted in the context of a two-sided civil war—one that the Tutsi were winning—rather than a one-sided, ethnic genocide against the Tutsi. Second, after a few days, violence was reported to be on the wane when in reality it was accelerating. Third, most early death counts were gross underestimates, sometimes by a factor of ten, and did not reach genocidal proportions. Fourth, the initial focus was almost exclusively on Kigali, a relatively small city, and failed to indicate the broader scope of violence. Fifth, no credible and knowledgeable observers, including human rights groups, raised the prospect that a genocide was under way until the end of the second week.

Civil War with the Tutsi Winning

Because the RPA resumed its offensive in the capital and from the north on the first day, renewed killing was reported in the context of a two-sided civil war. On April 11, an editorial in London's *Times* pondering international calls for a cease-fire asked rhetorically, "Which parties would be asked to cease fire against whom?" On April 12, a Belgian newspaper reported, "It is absolutely certain that a large number of acts of terror were committed [in rebel-controlled areas] too." The U.S. Committee for Refugees emphasized that the violence was "shamelessly political, not ethnic." In an April 15 report, UNAMIR commander Roméo Dallaire identified the problem as mutual violence, stating that the UN presence would be reassessed "if we see another three weeks of being cooped up and seeing them pound *each other.*" Interestingly, even many Rwandan Hutu did not immediately perceive the outbreak of civil violence as one-sided, so they too fled their homes in terror, returning only if and when the anti-Tutsi nature of violence in their region became clear. It is still unclear today how many Hutu were killed by Tutsi during the genocide and its aftermath—and, therefore, to what extent the initial reports of mutual killing were inaccurate.[5]

Also obscuring any notion of a centrally orchestrated genocide were repeated reports that the Rwandan Armed Forces (FAR) were not participating in massacres, a point confirmed by both the government and rebels at least through April 18. The government's motivation for such deception was obvious, to hide the FAR's role until the genocide could be completed. The RPF's incentive for such deception was less obvious, but apparently the rebel group was trying to lure moderate elements of the FAR into an alliance against the extremists and thus strove to avoid tagging them as murderers. For the first two weeks, rebel radio instead blamed the Presidential Guard and the interim government for being "largely responsible for the atrocities," and thereby created the impression that the bulk of government forces were not involved in massacres.[6]

Further contributing to the confusion of Western observers, the rebels had launched their own campaign of political assassination against Hutu opponents by April 9, both in Kigali and in the countryside. The interim government exploited this by exaggerating the abuses of the RPF, charging on April 15 that the rebels had massacred 20,000 people. A U.S. official recalls that in mid-April 1994, "We didn't know who was shooting at whom."[7]

Early reports also indicated that the Tutsi-led rebels were winning the civil war and rejecting government offers of a nationwide cease-fire, which contradicted any notion of Tutsi as victims. The rebels wanted a cease-fire only in the capital, where they were initially outgunned, but refused to halt their offensive in the countryside, where they were making rapid progress. By April 13 the Hutu interim government had fled Kigali for refuge in Gitarama, and a Paris radio station reported, "The fall of Kigali seems imminent." On April 14, European newspapers reported that Hutu now feared vengeance from Tutsi rebels who had gained the upper hand in Kigali. As Western troops arrived in Kigali during the first week to evacuate foreign nationals, a confident and suspicious RPF not only did not ask for assistance but also demanded that the troops depart immediately so as not to interfere with the rebels' imminent victory. Only on April 23 did the RPF propose a nationwide cease-fire, after two weeks of refusing such offers from the government.[8]

In explaining the rebels' belated cease-fire offer at the end of April, one account reported, "The rebels apparently see their self-declared truce as a 'last chance' offer to the government to rein in roving militia bands." The RPF rejected earlier cease-fire offers on the grounds that those making the offers would not or could not stop the massacres, which the rebels insisted on as a precondition for any cease-fire. However, that does not explain the rebels' later change of heart. One possibility is that the later shift was an insincere gesture intended only to persuade international audiences that the RPF was peace-loving. However, this is denied by Patrick Mazimhaka, then director of external affairs for the Rwandan Patriotic Front. He says the RPF's change of heart was motivated mainly by the belated realization that the rebels would not gain control of the western half of Rwanda before most Tutsi there were killed. The only hope of saving those Tutsi was an alliance with the FAR against the extremist government. The rebels hoped to win such an alliance by offering the FAR a cease-fire as an alternative to its impending military defeat.[9]

Violence Waning

Starting on April 11, just four days into the violence, news reports indicated that fighting in Rwanda had "diminished in intensity." Three days later it was reported that "a strange calm reigns in downtown" Kigali. By the following day, April 15, the calm had spread to the capital's suburbs, permitting "humanitarian organizations to cautiously resume their activities." The commander of Belgian peacekeepers in Rwanda confirmed: "The fighting has died down somewhat, one could say that it has all but stopped." As late as April 17, UNAMIR commander Dallaire told the BBC that except for an isolated pocket in the north, "the rest of the line is essentially quite quiet."[10]

Only on April 18 did a Belgian radio station question this consensus, explaining that the decline in reports of violence was because "most foreigners have left, including journalists." The exodus of reporters was so extreme that it virtually halted Western press coverage. European newspapers that initially had provided daily coverage of the violence started to ignore it on April 18. For example, France's *Le Monde* went silent for four days and Britain's *Guardian* for seven. Ironically, this was just as the killing peaked and spread to Rwanda's final two prefectures.[11]

Death Estimates Not on Genocidal Scale

Three days into the killing, on April 10, the *New York Times* quoted estimates of 8,000 dead in Kigali by the French humanitarian group Médecins Sans Frontières and "tens of thousands" by the International Committee of the Red Cross (ICRC). Three days later, the RPF offered its own estimate that "more than 20,000" were dead in Kigali.[12] However, during the second week, media estimates did not rise at all and so failed to approach levels that commonly would be considered "genocidal" for a country of 8 million people that included 650,000 Tutsi.

The definition of genocide in the 1948 UN convention says that it is the intent to destroy a group "in whole or in part," without any reference to the number killed, so in theory a single murder could be genocide.[13] However, in common usage "genocide" has come to denote the intentional destruction of a significant portion of a group's population. Death tolls of 20,000 are not uncommon in civil wars and generally are not considered genocidal. In order to make a determination of genocide in a specific case, one has to examine the details of the violence, including whether the victims were noncombatants, were killed deliberately (rather than in crossfire), were members of a single group defined by ascriptive characteristics, and were being targeted exclusively because of their identity rather than for suspected actions such as supporting antigovernment rebels. In the absence of such details, only a high death estimate would suggest the possibility of genocide. Accordingly, given the early confusion about the nature of the violence in Rwanda, a death toll of 20,000 during the first week did not seem to indicate the occurrence of genocide.

On April 16 the *Guardian* still reported only an "estimated 20,000 deaths." Two days later the *New York Times* repeated this statistic, underestimating the actual carnage at that point by about tenfold. Not until a few days later did the scope of killing rapidly emerge. On April 20, Human Rights Watch declared that "as many as 100,000 people may have died to date," and the RPF warned that "hundreds of thousands of defenseless" victims were being slaughtered. By the following day the ICRC too was estimating that perhaps "hundreds of thousands" were dead.[14] Ironically, these belated and sudden increases in death estimates may have raised skepticism among some Western officials at the time, because such estimates by human rights organizations in other conflicts—before and after the Rwanda tragedy—often have proved to be substantially inflated.[15]

Massacres Confined to the Capital

For nearly two weeks, news organizations, the UN, and NGOs focused almost exclusively on Kigali, failing to report the far broader tragedy unfolding outside the capital. Three main causes for this lapse can be identified. First, extremist Hutu engaged in a deliberate strategy of concealment. Second, there was a dearth of foreigners and reporters in the countryside as they migrated to the capital for evacuation during the first days, and those in Kigali were kept busy reporting on the city's chaos and the evacuation. Third, after completion of the evacuation on April 13, few foreigners remained anywhere in Rwanda. The resulting initial focus on Kigali, a city that contained only 4 percent of Rwanda's population, obscured the nationwide scope of violence and therefore its genocidal intent.

In retrospect, it is clear that sporadic reports of rural violence did emerge—uncovered by advancing rebel troops or reported by Westerners who evacuated from the countryside. However, these reports initially were too fragmented or distorted to reveal the true scope of killing. In perhaps the best early indication in an open source, the *Guardian* reported on April 11, in the final paragraphs of a report focused on the capital: "Stories of atrocities and violence elsewhere in the country are filtering into Kigali. . . . [A] Hutu extremist movement attacked a religious center in Kigufi, near the border with Zaire. They separated out all the Tutsis and killed them in front of the nuns and several expatriate aid workers."

France, Belgium, the United Nations, and at least one NGO also knew of some civilian massacres outside Kigali during the first week. On April 7, Belgium's defense intelligence agency observed that massacres were under way in Rwanda's "cities." Though this report did not indicate genocidal scope or intent, or even mention the rural areas where most Rwandans live, the reference to more than one urban area suggests that Belgian intelligence officials knew on the first day that violence went beyond Kigali. Likewise, on April 8, 1994, the French embassy in Washington, D.C., informed Belgian intelligence officials that massacres of Rwandan opposition politicians and Tutsi were occurring both inside and outside of Kigali.[16] Presumably France shared this information with U.S. officials as well. In addition, a Human Rights Watch official reports that UNAMIR personnel knew of massacres in Gisenyi, and possibly Cyangugu and Kibuye as well, before their departure from those areas on April 10 and 11, 1994. Some peacekeepers remained in Butare until April 20 and thus may also have been aware of massacres in Gikongoro and Butare. Reports by NGOs tended to focus mainly on Kigali during the first two weeks of violence, but one exception was an ICRC estimate of 20,000 dead on April 11, 1994, which indicated that only half were inside Kigali.[17]

However, most of these few early reports of rural violence seemed to indicate the renewal of mutual communal strife or civil war, rather than genocide. On April 11 a Paris radio station reported, "Hutus are hunting down Tutsis throughout the country" but added, "and the other way around." A Belgian radio station reported that killing and looting had spread to Cyangugu but identified the targets as the "opposition" rather than Tutsi. On April 12 the *Washington Post* reported that "sketchy reports said fighting has spread to Rwanda's countryside" but in a context suggesting organized combat between RPA and FAR troops. A Spanish radio station said several Rwandan nuns had claimed that Hutu in the countryside were threatening Tutsi and then killing them "if they didn't get what they wanted." This indicated some spread of looting and extortion, but did not suggest the wanton killing taking place in the capital. Moreover, the radio station itself conceded the lack of reliability of such early reports, prefacing its report with the caveat: "If a Rwandan human rights organization in Brussels is to be believed. . . ."[18]

Even an RPF official, interviewed by the BBC on April 12, seemed not to appreciate the scale of rural violence. Asked about fighting outside the capital, he discussed only the military progress of "forces" in the north and east and failed even to mention civilian victims in the countryside, stating: "We want to stop the senseless killing that is going on *in Kigali*." In following days, rebel radio began to report that "youthwingers" and retreating soldiers were engaged in killing outside the capital, but without any hint of the scale.[19]

The first individual reports of large-scale killing outside the capital came during the second week, on April 16, when newspapers around the world reported the massacre of 1,200 Tutsi "at a Church in Musha, 25 miles from Kigali." The same day, the RPF announced that 200 had been killed in the commune of Rukira in Kibungo prefecture, and the BBC reported corpses at checkpoints on the road from Kigali to Gitarama. On April 17, *Le Monde* reported 1,180 Tutsi "exterminated" in the village of Gikoro, about forty kilometers from Kigali, although this may have been a repeat of the report on nearby Musha. Two days later, Agence France Presse reported that about 800 corpses, "mostly Tutsi, hacked to death by government troops," had been found in a pit in Kaziguro in northeastern Rwanda.[20] The source of most of these initial reports appears to have been the RPA, which uncovered massacre sites and rescued survivors in the course of its rapid eastern offensive.

The nationwide scope of the killing first emerged around April 19, when rebel radio reported, "Gitarama, Butare, Gikongoro, and Kibuye prefectures have now fallen victim to the massacres, as is the case for the capital, Kigali." At the same time, the RPF accused the interim Hutu government of being "determined to exterminate sections of the population." More cautious, the U.S. Committee for Refugees characterized events in the countryside as "extremely unclear" but warned that the reported "shift of violence to rural regions is ominous, since most Rwandans live in rural areas." By April 21, Belgian radio confirmed that Butare, "which until now had been miraculously preserved from the massacres, is now getting its full dose."[21]

American newspapers failed to convey the nationwide scope of the violence until April 22, when they belatedly reported that fighting bands had reduced "much of the country to chaos." Still, many foreign observers could not conceive that a genocide was under way. On April 23, the *Washington Post* reported that international aid workers, pondering why only 20,000 refugees had crossed the border while a half-million Tutsi had fled their homes, concluded that "most of the borders have been sealed by the Rwandan Army." Only on April 25 did the *New York Times* solve the riddle, reporting that violence had "widened into what appears to be a methodical killing of Tutsi across the countryside." The missing refugees "either have been killed or are trying to hide," it reported, based on the testimony of survivors who had escaped to Burundi.

The media were not alone in failing to perceive the true scope of violence. Officials of Human Rights Watch, in op-ed articles published on April 14 and April 17, provided no hint of an attempted nationwide genocide. As late as April 20, UN Secretary General Boutros Boutros-Ghali described the killings as "mainly in Kigali."[22]

No Early Claims of "Genocide"

The most compelling evidence that President Clinton could not have reached an early determination of attempted genocide is that not even human rights organizations or the rebels themselves did so. The political opposition in Kigali did claim as early as April 10 that extremist Hutu were trying to "exterminate the Tutsi minority" in the city. However, this accusation was limited to activities in the capital and conflicted with simultaneous reports that Kigali's Hutu feared for their lives because Tutsi rebels were poised to capture the city.[23] Only on April 17 did RPF radio declare, "The world cannot and should not forget the genocide which is being perpetrated in Rwanda today," a report translated and published by the CIA on April 19.[24] However, rebel claims alone would not have been sufficient to trigger U.S. action because such claims are viewed with skepticism on grounds that they sometimes are concocted in hopes of garnering international support and intervention.[25] The first Western organization to raise the prospect was Human Rights Watch, also on April 19, in a letter to the UN Security Council, stating: "Rwandan military authorities are engaged in a systematic campaign to eliminate the Tutsi . . . so concerted that we believe it constitutes genocide." The group went public with the charge in a press release the following day. Other international observers, however, were considerably more cautious. The Pope first used the word genocide on April 27. The U.S. Committee for Refugees waited until May 2 to urge the Clinton administration to make such a determination. Only on May 4 did the UN secretary general finally declare a "real genocide."[26]

To summarize, neither the media, the UN, human rights organizations, nor the Tutsi rebels themselves initially appreciated the nationwide scope and genocidal nature of the violence. Nearly two weeks into it, reports suggested that only 20,000 Rwandans had been killed by both sides in a civil war that the Tutsi were winning, that was confined mainly to the capital, and in which violence was waning. Only on April 17 did the rebels start using the term genocide regularly, and only on April 19 did they report massacres occurring across the country. In the West, genocide was first invoked by a human rights organization on April 19, and large death estimates emerged only the following day. The *New York Times* did not report a nationwide extermination campaign until April 25.

Of course, on the basis of numerous early-warning indicators in press accounts, diplomatic traffic, reports from nongovernmental organizations, and UN cables, many close observers had feared a renewal of large-scale violence in Rwanda for months or years before the genocide. Despite those early warnings, however, these same close observers did not immediately perceive the outbreak of violence in Rwanda as the beginning of genocide. Several explanations for this "warning-response" failure are discussed in chapter 10, but the most important appears to be that the experts were focused on a different risk—that extremists would use a few circumscribed massacres to undermine the implementation of the Arusha peace agreement and spark a renewal of the civil war in Rwanda. Indeed, before the genocide, leading West-ern academics and human rights organizations stressed that the underlying cause of conflict in Rwanda was politics, not ancient ethnic hatred. Thus when violence exploded in the capital, these experts perceived it through the prism of their expectations as the renewal of civil war. Though some experts may claim in retrospect that they immediately perceived the violence as genocide, the concurrent historical record does not support these assertions. In fact, the possibility of genocide was not raised publicly until physical evidence of the killing campaign began to emerge.

Classified Intelligence

One U.S. government organization, the Defense Intelligence Agency, obtained special intelligence about Rwanda soon after the renewal of violence indicating somewhat earlier than April 20 that anti-Tutsi killing was wide-spread and likely to grow to large numbers, according to a senior DIA Africa analyst at the time. Within 24 hours of Habyarimana's plane being shot down, the DIA had requested and obtained satellite photos and communication intercepts as part of its preparation for the evacuation of embassy officials and other U.S. nationals from Rwanda (known formally as a "noncombatant evacuation order," or NEO). The deployment of such national technical means of gathering intelligence is controlled by the Central Intelligence Agency, but the DIA "got all the intelligence assets we asked for," according to the analyst, because of the priority assigned to protecting American nationals. In addition, the U.S. defense attaché based in Cameroon—the sole human intelligence asset in the region—was in Rwanda during the renewal of violence and pro-vided valuable information, according to the DIA analyst.[27]

The intended purpose of this gathering of intelligence was to determine the level of danger to American nationals and the best means and routes to evac-uate them. However, within 24 hours, the communications intercepts also revealed that Rwandan officials in Kigali were sending orders to their coun-terparts in outlying areas of the country to kill Tutsi. Within 48 to 72 hours, the DIA intercepted replies from some local officials indicating that they had accomplished their assigned missions. Simultaneously, satellite photos con-firmed the existence of several specific massacre sites inside and outside Kigali. (DIA officials had directed the satellites to take photos of Kigali, as well as other cities and areas suspected of massacres based on the intercepted communica-tions.) Further confirmation was provided by the Tutsi rebels, who were coming across massacre sites as they advanced south and east; the senior DIA analyst was in daily communication with the rebel leadership. On the basis of this intelligence, the DIA made extrapolations of the number of Tutsi already killed, predicted that the number was likely to rise, and regularly updated these estimates. In addition, the DIA regularly prepared maps indicating the location of the massacres, as well as the positions of government and rebel troops and any combat between them, and distributed these classified maps and estimates to other relevant U.S. government agencies. The other executive branch and intelligence agencies, however, disagreed with these extreme DIA estimates at the time, and explicitly noted this disagreement in intelligence summaries prepared for senior officials and the president.[28]

There are several plausible explanations for why the DIA's proprietary intelligence was not incorporated or utilized by other parts of the national security establishment in Washington. The main cause may be nothing more complicated or sinister than an overload of information. During the first week of violence and implementation of the NEO, officials in Washington received as many as a thousand separate intelligence reports on Rwanda *per day*—from the media, NGOs, foreign embassies, the UN, and multiple U.S. intelligence agencies. "The circuits were overwhelmed," according to the State Department intelligence official for Rwanda at the time. "It was a complete 'fog of war' type situation."[29]

One coping mechanism among veteran Washington intelligence officials faced with such information overload is to dismiss extreme, unconfirmed reports. Apparently, this is what happened with the DIA reports, because none of the senior U.S. officials interviewed for this book who worked on Rwanda during the genocide at the NSC, State Department, and Pentagon has any recollection of ever seeing such reports. These officials include some who are quite critical of the U.S. government's lack of response in Rwanda and its unwillingness to acknowledge the genocide after it came to light in late April 1994 and who therefore would appear to have no motivation to falsely deny the existence of such reports. However, neither does the DIA analyst appear to have an incentive to lie about his early warnings, because he does not claim that quick U.S. intervention based on his warnings could have stopped the genocide and civil war. (Once the violence erupted, he concludes bluntly, "military intervention would not have been able to stop it.") Moreover, senior officials elsewhere in the Pentagon and at other departments vouch for this analyst's veracity. Accordingly, they concede that the DIA reports might have existed and even crossed their desks but note that a single extreme claim probably would not have made a big impact on them in the face of the welter of other information they were receiving, mainly from open sources.[30] Indeed, most U.S. officials who covered Rwanda at the time have no recollection of receiving any significant proprietary intelligence at all. One State Department official who participated in a special round-the-clock interagency task force established after Habyarimana's death is typical in stating that, "We had CNN on . . . I don't recall us knowing anything that was not already being reported by the press."[31]

A second possible reason that this proprietary intelligence had little impact was skepticism on several grounds concerning the DIA's reporting. First, the senior DIA analyst was known to be close to the Tutsi-led rebels in Rwanda, so that other U.S. agencies may have dismissed his extreme claims about the killing of Tutsi as mere RPF propaganda. Indeed, the DIA analyst was aware that this impression existed, and a State Department intelligence official confirms it. Second, this problem was compounded by the DIA's inability to reveal its sources and methods because of standard government restrictions. Thus, officials were presented only with the DIA's extreme conclusions—without knowing they were based on intercepted Rwandan government communications. Third, other agencies were unconvinced by the DIA's photographic analysis techniques, which included estimating the number killed within buildings by the number of corpses in surrounding courtyards and extrapolating nationwide death estimates from a few scattered massacres. While the DIA had confidence in these extrapolations, in part because of confirming evidence in the communications it intercepted, other agencies were more skeptical and insisted on photographic or other hard evidence of the death count at each alleged massacre site. Finally, other agencies may have been skeptical simply because it was hard for anyone to believe that the massacres could be so large and widespread, especially so quickly.[32]

A third possible explanation for the failure of other agencies to accept the early DIA reporting is that they had a cognitive or motivated bias against it. At the Pentagon during the first week, the Africa office was planning the NEO and thus was obsessed with intelligence pertaining to the safety of Americans—civilians and evacuation troops—which may explain why officials there don't remember reports from their own intelligence agency about the growing threat to Rwandans.[33] At the State Department and NSC, the regional diplomatic preoccupation during the first days of violence was to avoid a renewal of the civil war that U.S. diplomats had spent several years bringing to a negotiated conclusion at Arusha. In this context, U.S. officials may not have wanted to believe accusations of widespread killing of Tutsi because such violence would give a green light to the RPF to renew the war. Indeed, this fits with the admission of a former NSC official that the U.S. administration's goal was "to keep the FAR in their barracks to avoid the restart of civil war."[34]

Ironically, the administration's greatest fear of civil violence in the region during the first week was a posible contagion effect in Burundi, which had suffered large-scale ethnic violence only six months earlier and was considered more susceptible than Rwanda.[35] Looking for reports of mass killing in Burundi, NSC officials apparently gave inadequate attention to such reports about Rwanda. Additionally, in the wake of the Somalia debacle just six months earlier, the entire U.S. government had a strong bias against any new humanitarian military interventions. It is possible that U.S. officials, consciously or otherwise, dismissed initial reports of large-scale violence in Rwanda because such information would have raised the prospect of another UN or U.S. humanitarian intervention that they plainly did not want to contemplate.[36]

A last possible reason that the DIA's early reports failed to alert the rest of Washington to the emerging genocide has to do with the details and framing of their content. During the first two weeks, the DIA never alleged that "genocide" was occurring. In addition, although the DIA had intercepted multiple communications from Kigali to local Rwandan officials to carry out their orders, the agency never obtained any "smoking gun" evidence of an overarching plan to kill all Tutsi and thus never reported such a plot. Further, the DIA's gathering of intelligence dropped off substantially by the end of the first week for two reasons: the completion of the NEO and the retreat of the extremist Hutu government to Gitarama, which interrupted government communications to local officials. Last, although the DIA analyst now claims that he believed during the first days of violence that the death toll would spiral to very high numbers, the figures in his reports at the time were limited to the significantly lower estimates of victims already killed. It is possible that if the DIA reports had projected during the first few days that hundreds of thousands of Tutsi would soon be killed, other government agencies might have taken greater note.[37]

Although it remains unclear which of these causes was principally responsible for the failure of the American government to process adequately the DIA intelligence, what is clear is that this proprietary intelligence was not incorporated or utilized by key elements of the U.S. national security bureaucracy. Confirmation is provided by an informal NSC study conducted after the genocide to determine the sources of intelligence failure in Rwanda. The study reviewed reports and cables prepared by U.S. officials working in the NSC, the United Nations, and Rwanda at the time. According to a former NSC official, this review did not uncover any early reports by the DIA of large-scale killing of Tutsi, which indicates that these reports did not register with other U.S. officials then working on Rwanda. Most classified cables and reports from the period instead referred to "communal violence," a term that suggested decentralized and mutual violence rather than genocide.[38]

Further evidence of the failure of Washington to absorb the DIA intelligence is provided by the recollections of other U.S. officials who worked on Rwanda. A former senior NSC director, who decries the U.S. failure to intervene after the genocide became apparent in late April, nevertheless insists that "during the first couple of weeks our perception was not that mass killings were taking place." Instead, he and his colleagues initially believed that the extremists' attacks were circumscribed and targeted mainly at the political leadership of the Tutsi and moderate Hutu. During the first few days, this official says he met with Human Rights Watch representatives who requested action to stop hate radio, protect specific individuals in Rwanda, and prevent the withdrawal of UN troops. However, he insists that these human rights officials did not warn of impending genocide at the time, "regardless of what the group claims now." According to the NSC official, "It was only toward April 20th or 22nd that we started to get reports from human rights groups that the extremists weren't just going after high-level individuals, which was our perception."[39]

Similarly, the State Department intelligence official then responsible for Rwanda reports that for two weeks he did not perceive that an orchestrated mass-killing campaign was under way. Indeed, during the first week he received reports from the NEO mission that the Rwandan countryside was fairly calm. These reports were true at the time, because the evacuation route used by the mission led south through Gitarama and Butare prefectures—the last to be consumed by genocide. This official insists that he did not comprehend the extent of killing until around April 23–25. Specifically, he remembers being jarred into awareness not by any proprietary intelligence, but by an alarming report from the usually conservative ICRC, which estimated that more than 100,000 already had been killed in Rwanda.[40] The Pentagon's then-director for Africa likewise concurs that he and other informed officials within the U.S. government became aware of the genocide about "two weeks in."[41] There is good reason to believe that these recollections are sincere and not merely post hoc rationalizations for U.S. inaction, because these officials also criticize the U.S. government for failing to acknowledge the genocide after evidence of it did become clear.

In conclusion, it appears that the DIA did have access to proprietary intelligence that strongly suggested within the first week that large numbers of Tutsi were being targeted and killed in several areas of Rwanda. However, the key agencies in Washington—the State Department, Pentagon, NSC, and CIA—

either failed to absorb this information or explicitly rejected it as unreliable and thus did not become aware of the genocide until further evidence emerged on or after April 20. Even the DIA's own reports before this date did not mention the possibility of genocide or predict that hundreds of thousands of Tutsi eventually would be killed. Moreover, the early intelligence summaries prepared for the president—which he may or may not have read—explicitly stated that the other agencies disagreed with the worst-case assessments of the DIA.

This phenomenon, in which the best information fails to reach government decisionmakers, has been noted in another context by former senator Daniel Patrick Moynihan, an eight-year member of the U.S. Senate Select Committee on Intelligence. Writing about the intelligence community's failure to predict the fall of the Soviet Union, he concludes: "If some individual CIA analysts were more prescient than the corporate view, their ideas were filtered out in the bureaucratic process; and it is the corporate view that counts because that is what reaches the president and his advisers."[42] For the same reason, it is unreasonable to argue that President Clinton could have made a determination of genocide before his senior experts on Rwanda had reached this conclusion and before he was presented with strong evidence that such a campaign was under way. Accordingly, the earliest that the president realistically could have made a determination of attempted genocide in Rwanda was about April 20, 1994, or two weeks into the violence.

CHAPTER FIVE

The Military

Scene

At the time of President Juvénal Habyarimana's assassination, Rwanda hosted three military forces, those of the government, the rebels, and the United Nations. Government forces totaled about 40,000, including army, national police (*gendarmerie*), and the 1,500-man Presidential Guard (PG). Except for the PG and a few other elite battalions, however, this force was largely hollow, having expanded sixfold in three years in response to the rebel threat. The government conscripted young, unemployed Rwandans without skills and gave them only rudimentary training, assisted by France. From 1990 to 1994, the Rwandan Armed Forces (FAR) grew from approximately 5,200 to more than 30,000 active-duty forces, and the gendarmerie from 2,000 to 6,000. France promoted the expansion to enable Rwandan government forces to fend off the rebels without the assistance of French troops, a strategy of "Rwandanization." The original smaller gendarmerie had been well trained by France and Germany, but its new recruits were virtually untrained. The elite Presidential Guard was recruited almost exclusively from northwestern Rwanda, Habyarimana's home region, and was trained by France and Israel.[1]

Another 15,000 to 30,000 Hutu around the country participated in militias during the genocide, but many apparently did not possess firearms or ammunition. Militias first emerged in Rwanda in the early 1990s as a consequence of President Habyarimana's initial steps toward political pluralization. The president's party, as well as opposition parties, formed lightly armed youth wings—each with a different name—which engaged each other in violence and intimidation. As the civil war against the RPF intensified, the government and Hutu extremists took three steps to change the nature of these militias in preparation for genocide: persuading opposition parties that their militias should focus not against the government but against Tutsi; establishing an additional "self-defense force" militia ostensibly unassociated with any political party; and providing formal military training to the militia of Habyarimana's MRND Party, the Interahamwe ("Those who work or fight together"), and that of the extremist CDR Party, the Impuzamugambi ("Those with a single purpose"). The other militias were the MDR's Inkuba ("Thunder"), the PSD's Abakambozi ("Liberators"), and the Jeunesse Libéral ("Liberal Youth") of the Parti Libéral (PL). France helped train the militias, assuming they would join the FAR in combating the rebel invasion, although only a few thousand of these militia were reported to have received any formal military training before the genocide. France also armed them indirectly by providing weapons to the FAR with instructions to pass along a portion to the militias. Once the genocide began, militia ranks swelled to the cited level of between 15,000 and 30,000. Some of the opposition-party militias initially refused to take part in the genocide campaign, but after their leaders were killed or removed from positions of authority by the government, they apparently joined in the genocide to such an extent that their activities became virtually indistinguishable from those of the original extremists. Accordingly, Rwandans sometimes refer to the militias generically as Interahamwe.[2]

The varying degrees of quality and political extremism among Rwanda's Hutu forces have been characterized by UNAMIR's deputy commander, General Henry Anyidoho of Ghana: "The state of morale in the Rwandan government forces was noticeably low before the [renewal of] war . . . a state of disarray. . . . The Presidential Guards were viewed as soldiers of the elite regiment, whereas the majority of the regular forces were ignored . . . were alienated and were not committed to the cause of the government." The army "did not appear to have any in-depth political education. It was the murderous militia that had the strong political indoctrination."[3]

The quantities of FAR armaments reported in open-source literature of the period are likely underestimates, given that troop levels are underreported in the same sources. However, these sources correctly describe the modest quality of the Rwandan government's military equipment. Rebel arms were

Table 5-1. *Relative Manpower, April 1994*

Rwandan Armed Forces (FAR)/Hutu		Rwandan Patriotic Army (RPA)/Tutsi[a]		UNAMIR Peacekeepers	
Army	30,000–40,000	Rebels	20,000–25,000	Belgians	420
Presidential				Non-western	2,100
Guard	1,500				
National Police	6,000				
Subtotal	approx. 40,000				
Militia[b]	15,000–30,000				
Total	**55,000–70,000**		**20,000–25,000**		**2,500**

Sources: Manpower estimates are drawn from various sources (see text).

a. As noted in the text, the RPA was dominated by Tutsi refugees but included some Hutu and was politically allied with elements of the domestic Hutu opposition.

b. Militia figures are estimates. Only a few thousand militia had received any formal military training.

even more primitive and included few motorized vehicles and no air assets (see tables 5-1 and 5-2).

UNAMIR had three infantry battalions authorized under Chapter VI of the UN charter, meaning their presence was subject to the consent of the Rwandan government. Rules of engagement were somewhat ambiguous but generally were interpreted to bar use of force except in self-defense or in joint operations with Rwandan national police.[4] The peacekeeping force was built around a small 420-man Belgian battalion in Kigali, reinforced with 400 Ghanaian troops and accompanied by about 600 logistics, engineering, medical, and headquarters personnel. In addition, near the demilitarized zone in northern Rwanda, a Ghanaian battalion monitored the RPA in Byumba prefecture, while a Bangladeshi battalion monitored the FAR in Ruhengeri prefecture—together employing about 1,000 peacekeepers. Another 100 UN observers were stationed in southern Uganda, intended to ensure that arms did not flow to the rebels, a mission of questionable effectiveness.[5] Finally, a handful of UN observers were distributed elsewhere around the country in Gisenyi, Kibuye, Cyangugu, and Butare.[6] Overall, UNAMIR had about 2,500 troops (see figure 5-1).

On the first day of violence the Presidential Guard executed ten Belgian peacekeepers who were attempting to protect Rwanda's opposition prime minister. These deaths and the emerging chaos in Kigali prompted Western governments to launch an emergency evacuation of their nationals. Early on the morning of April 9 some 190 French paratroopers landed and seized control of Kigali airport; they were later reinforced by several hundred more French troops, to begin Operation Amaryllis. The next day, 450 Belgian and

Table 5-2. *Rwandan Armed Forces (FAR) Equipment*

Equipment	Number
Army	
Armored vehicles	
M-3 armored personnel carriers	16
AML-60 light armored vehicles	12
AML-90 light armored vehicles	?
VBL M-11 reconnaissance	16
Artillery	
122 mm D-30 howitzers	>6
105 mm LG1 howitzers	9
Mortars	
120 mm mortars	>6
81–82 mm mortars	28
60 mm mortars	>100
Heavy guns	
75 mm cannons (recoilless rifles)	?
57 mm ATK guns	6
37 mm guns	?
Rocket launchers	
83 mm rocket launchers	?
40 mm grenade launchers	>70
Aviation	
Helicopters	
SA-316 Aerospatiale Alouettes	7
SA-342L Aerospatiale Gazelles	6
Armed or attack helicopters	0
Fixed-wing aircraft	
C-47 Douglas Dakotas	2
Do 27Q-4 Dornier propeller airplanes	1
Britten-Norman Islanders	2
R-235 counterinsurgency airplanes	2
Civil aviation airplanes	2
Air defense	
Missiles	
SA-7 (reported)	?
Antiaircraft artillery	
37 mm guns	?

Sources: *The Military Balance 1993–1994* (London: International Institute for Strategic Studies, 1993); Stephen D. Goose and Frank Smyth, "Arming Genocide in Rwanda," *Foreign Affairs* (September/October 1994), 86–96; Frank Smyth, *Arming Rwanda* (New York: Human Rights Watch Arms Project, 1994); Ntaribi Kamanzi, *Rwanda: Du Génocide à la Défaite* (Kigali: Editions Rebero, 1997); and *SIPRI Yearbook 1995* (Oxford: Oxford University Press, 1995).

Figure 5-1. *UNAMIR Peacekeepers in Rwanda before the Genocide*

80 Italian troops arrived for Operation Silverback. UNAMIR arranged a forty-eight-hour guarantee from the warring factions not to interfere with the evacuation. By April 13 these troops had evacuated virtually all of Rwanda's several thousand Westerners—except those of the International Committee of the Red Cross and Médecins Sans Frontières—and had departed themselves. The next day, Belgium announced it also would be withdrawing its UNAMIR battalion, which triggered unease among the other troop-contributors and led the UN Security Council a week later to cut authorized troop levels to a skeleton crew of 270 (although the number of peacekeepers actually deployed never dipped below 456).[7]

Rebel forces, estimated at 20,000 upon the renewal of violence, had been constrained by the Arusha accords to a small area of northern Rwanda, except for the one authorized Kigali battalion, which the RPF had reinforced clandestinely to about 1,000 troops.[8] When civil war was renewed on April 7, the northern-based rebels set out in four directions. One group moved quickly south to reinforce the battalion in the capital, met little organized resistance, and arrived by April 11 or 12, compelling the interim government to retreat

Figure 5-2. *Rwandan Patriotic Front (RPF) Offensive, April–July 1994*

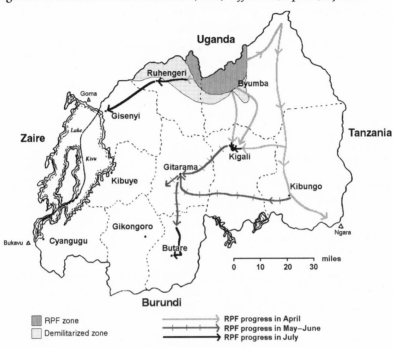

southwest to Gitarama on April 13, although the Rwandan army stayed to protect the capital. A second group made a rapid sweep east and then south through eastern Rwanda, with some splitting off halfway and turning west toward Kigali in mid-April and the rest continuing southeast to reach Tanzania's border by April 22, before turning west to capture southern Rwanda. A third group engaged the FAR in Byumba, following the April 12 withdrawal of peacekeepers from the north, defeated the Rwandan garrison there in about ten days, and proceeded to Kigali. A final group of rebels headed west and fought an initially deadlocked struggle against FAR forces in Ruhengeri, where the government had its largest concentration of troops outside Kigali.[9] Thus from late April until the end of June the war had two stationary fronts, in Kigali and Ruhengeri, and a broad mobile front moving westward through southern Rwanda. As the rebels advanced, Tutsi refugees from other countries as well as Tutsi from rebel-occupied Rwanda flocked to join the rebel cause. In just three months the rebels captured most of the country—Gitarama on June 9, Kigali on July 4, Butare on July 5, Ruhengeri on July 14, and Gisenyi on July 17—and declared a cease-fire on July 18, 1994 (see figure 5-2).[10]

As reports of genocide reached the outside world in late April, public outcry spurred the United Nations to reauthorize a beefed-up "UNAMIR II" on May 17. During the following month, however, the UN was unable to obtain any substantial contributions of troops and equipment. As a result, on June 22 the Security Council authorized France to lead its own intervention, Operation Turquoise.[11] Although the French-led operation did not occur until most Tutsi already were dead, it offers important insights into the potential for an earlier humanitarian military intervention.

Operation Turquoise

The genesis of France's Operation Turquoise and its precise original intent are still debated despite journalistic, scholarly, and government inquiries, in part because it was the outgrowth of bureaucratic political competition. As Graham Allison has observed famously about government decisionmaking: "Large acts result from innumerable and often conflicting smaller actions by individuals at various levels of bureaucratic organizations in the service of a variety of only partially compatible conceptions of national goals, organizational goals, and political objectives." Likewise, Morton Halperin has noted that bureaucracies use two opportunities to shape government policy to their own interests: first as it is being formulated, and second when they implement what was an ostensibly final decision.[12]

Elements of France's defense establishment clearly wanted to help their erstwhile ally, the Rwandan army, reverse its losses in the civil war. Once atrocities came to light, however, President François Mitterrand of France opposed overt assistance to the FAR. Still, the French president sought to block a victory by rebels he viewed as representing only the Tutsi minority. He even briefly considered a military occupation of the entire country until informed by his staff that it was unfeasible. Ultimately, France's decision to intervene was compelled by French public outcry over continuing reports of anti-Tutsi atrocities. Thus, ironically, Turquoise was triggered by concern for the Tutsi but implemented by a French military establishment hoping to help the Hutu.[13]

Human Rights Watch reports that elements within the French defense establishment managed to funnel small amounts of arms and advice to the Hutu army from the outbreak of renewed fighting in April 1994. The first shipment of weapons and military advisers for the FAR during the genocide actually accompanied the French evacuation mission to Kigali immediately after the outbreak of violence. Five additional arms shipments were transported from France to Rwanda through Zaire in May and June 1994. Such military assistance during the genocide was coordinated by a retired French officer who operated out of the French embassy in Kigali and was paid by the French government. Even as late as June 1994, French military officials still hoped to stem the FAR's losses sufficiently to lay the groundwork for renewed peace negotiations between the Hutu government and the Tutsi rebels.[14]

At its peak, Operation Turquoise comprised about 2,900 French military personnel—including 1,200 combat troops—and 500 troops from seven African states. Equipment included 100 armored vehicles, 600 other motorized vehicles, 10 helicopters, and 12 combat aircraft. Because Rwanda is landlocked and speed was at a premium, all troops and equipment were airlifted to the theater. First to deploy were specialized French troops, who were already located at French bases in Africa. Their prepositioning in Africa provided a "precious time savings," according to an official French military account. Also facilitating a quick deployment, the first echelon was mobilized a week early and lifted to Rwanda's border on June 21, before receiving UN authorization. France was prepared to act even without such authorization, but ultimately this vanguard entered Rwanda on June 23, the day following UN approval. Support troops followed from France. Three staging bases were employed— at Bangui, Central African Republic; Ndjamena, Chad; and Libreville, Gabon—all within 1,500 miles of Rwanda.[15]

The main theater airfield was Goma, Zaire, bordering northwestern Rwanda, which accepted midsize aircraft immediately and was upgraded rapidly to accept a limited number of wide bodies. A smaller airfield at Bukavu, Zaire, on Rwanda's southwestern border, accommodated tactical aircraft, which typically carried cargo that had been transloaded from larger aircraft at Goma. Combat aircraft operated from Kisangani, Zaire.[16]

The airlift during the two-month mission brought in about 9,000 short tons of cargo, of which 1,000 tons was humanitarian assistance. Although the mission's objective ostensibly was humanitarian, French equipment indicated that its troops were prepared for combat (see Table 5-3). The airlift was hindered by two main obstacles: Goma's primitive airfield and a severe regional shortage of aviation fuel. The strategic (long-distance) portion of the lift relied on leased Russian Antonov and Ilyushin aircraft, because Air France planes were unavailable or unable to land at Goma's unimproved runway.[17]

As French troops arrived, the Rwandan army still controlled the western half of Rwanda, but the rebels were making rapid progress. Some in Paris wanted French troops to stem any further FAR losses and establish an east-west partition, but the size and pattern of French deployment suggests this strategy was not pursued aggressively. French troops established their main

Table 5-3. *Statistics for Operation Turquoise*

Equipment/Statistic	Number
Ground forces	
Troops	3,400
Armored vehicles	100
120 mm marine mortar battery	1
Other vehicles	600
Aviation	
Helicopters	
Super Puma (heavy)	8
Gazelle (light)	2
Fixed-wing tactical aircraft	
Mirage F1CT ground attack	4
Mirage F1CR reconnaissance	4
Jaguar strike/fighter	4
Tactical-lift aircraft	
C-130	6
Transall	9
Strategic-lift aircraft	
Airbus (chartered)	1
Boeing 747 (chartered)	1
Antonov An-124 (chartered)	2
Ilyushin Il-76 (chartered)	?
Cargo airlifted	
Tons (for entire mission)	9,000
Ratio in Safe Humanitarian Zone	
Force/population (1,000s)	1.4
Force/area (square miles)	0.9
Helicopters/area (square miles)	0.005
Helicopters/population (1,000s)	0.007

Sources: Prunier, *The Rwanda Crisis*, p. 291; Minear and Guillot, *Soldiers to the Rescue*, p. 95; Vaccaro, "The Politics of Genocide," p. 386; Lanxade, "L'opération Turquoise."

base in Goma, Zaire, and then entered government-controlled Rwanda via Goma and Bukavu. Three tactical bases were established in southwestern Rwanda from which a few forays were made to protect and evacuate groups of threatened Rwandans. Soon after their entry, however, French troops were shocked by the feeble condition of the Rwandan army and the gruesome nature of anti-Tutsi carnage. When many realized they had been misled about the true nature of the civil war, they lost sympathy for the Hutu forces.[18]

Officially, the initial French goals were to establish a presence, then move to stop massacres, extract extremists, and protect the general population in southwestern Rwanda, where the RPF had not yet reached and genocide continued. Some have suggested that the French entry into northwestern Rwanda was intended to bolster the FAR militarily. However, despite pleas from the FAR and from Rwanda's Hutu government for French support and an expansion of the French occupation zone to include northwestern Rwanda, France refused. This disappointed and angered Hutu military and political leaders who, in the absence of such aid, felt compelled to flee to Zaire. The French troops departed northwestern Rwanda within two weeks of their arrival, by July 5. A simpler and less conspiratorial explanation for their original entry into northwestern Rwanda is that it was adjacent to the main French air base at Goma, Zaire, and therefore the easiest route into the country.[19]

The RPF still perceived the French troops as enemies marching eastward, and so the rebels accelerated their advance westward to halt them. Paris, seeking to avert this impending confrontation, presented a plan to the UN Security Council to establish a Safe Humanitarian Zone (SHZ) in southwestern Rwanda, which would circumscribe the area of French control but authorize force to prevent the rebels from entering. While the plan was essentially humanitarian in intent, it also resembled a scaled-down version of partition.

The RPF was highly suspicious and sought to test the will and intentions of France by luring some troops into an ambush July 3 on the road between Butare and Gikongoro. After a brief firefight, the two sides apparently agreed on the dimensions of the SHZ, which received UN authorization the next day.[20] The triangle-shaped zone was demarcated by the French bases already established in Rwanda—at Cyangugu (about 450 troops), Gikongoro (increased from 200 to 600 troops), and Kibuye (800 troops)—and supported by the rear base at Goma that had 1,300 troops (see figure 5-3).[21]

Some observers have speculated that a deal was cut in which the rebels accepted the SHZ in return for France's commitment not to assist the FAR in northwestern Rwanda.[22] However, the evidence suggests that France had already abandoned any intention of supporting the FAR in northwestern Rwanda by the end of the operation's first week, several days before the July 3 confrontation with the RPF. Although France has been criticized for using the cover of a humanitarian intervention to abet the extremist Hutu, in some regards France actually tricked the Hutu, taking advantage of their false expectation of significant military assistance to ensure that French troops would be

Figure 5-3. *Operation Turquoise: Bases and Safe Humanitarian Zone (SHZ)*

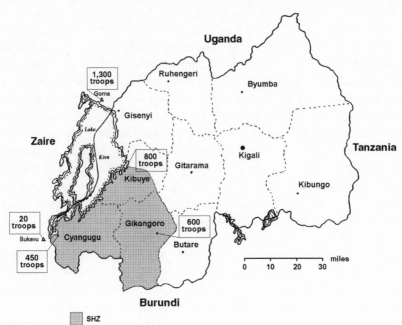

welcomed into Rwanda, then refusing to provide such aid. As a French military official acknowledges, deploying the operation "would have been hard without the cooperation of Rwandan government officials."[23]

Despite the hope that establishing an SHZ would prevent military confrontation, at least two more firefights broke out between French and rebel troops, on July 8 and July 17. An official French military history describes the incidents as its troops "encountering and repulsing the RPF." However, the rebels claim that in one incident French troops ventured outside the SHZ accompanied by FAR and militia forces, crossing rebel lines and prompting the RPF to attack and pursue them back into the zone. The rebels reportedly killed several Rwandan forces and captured eighteen of the French troops, even though the French had tried to stay out of the firefight. According to this account, the French captives were released on the order of General Paul Kagame, the head of the RPF, only after French commanders threatened to retaliate with air power.[24] Thus the rebels apparently were not afraid to confront French troops with force but were leery of a full-blown military confrontation, which led the rebels to accept a circumscribed French presence.

Because of the relatively small number of troops in Operation Turquoise, its capabilities were limited. The SHZ encompassed approximately 20 percent of Rwanda, or 2,000 square miles, with a population reduced by refugee outflow to between 1.2 and 1.5 million.[25] Up to 1,800 foreign troops were deployed inside the zone, representing less than 1.5 troops per thousand of population and less than one troop per square mile. Nevertheless, such sparsely deployed troops still had various capabilities:

—They generally could deter or defend themselves against attack.

—They could find and protect large concentrations of Tutsi who had not yet been slaughtered. However, it seems that only one such cluster was still surviving by the time of the intervention, a group of 8,000–12,000 refugees at Nyarushishi camp in Cyangugu who were discovered on the first day of the operation.

—They could sometimes find and protect small groups of threatened Tutsi in the countryside. However, this mission was not pursued aggressively for three reasons: a shortage of troops, an initial French belief that Hutu were the victims, and false warnings by local officials that murderous Tutsi rebels lurked in the southwestern countryside. In reality, the RPF had not yet reached the area and it was Hutu who were killing in the countryside. Such false Hutu claims help explain the initial French delay in trying to stop the killing of Tutsi in, for example, Bisesero, Kibuye—often cited by human rights groups critical of French behavior because of the many Tutsi who died there during Operation Turquoise. A senior officer in Operation Turquoise claims that the killing of Tutsi in the SHZ ceased about a week after the arrival of French troops, but in all likelihood it continued at lower levels for several more weeks.[26]

French patrols sometimes encountered pockets of endangered Tutsi in the course of their other duties but typically lacked sufficient troops and vehicles to conduct an immediate rescue. They promised to return with reinforcements in a few days, but by that time many of the Tutsi were dead. African Rights describes such a scenario in both Gikongoro and Kibuye and claims that "the killings continued in many remote parts of Kibuye and Cyangugu right through to August." Prunier describes the same phenomenon and offers an explanation: "There were too many useless armoured cars and not enough trucks because the whole operation had been conceived as a fighting one." Interestingly, the French used helicopters to search for large concentrations of Rwandan refugees, who were mainly Hutu, but do not appear to have looked for smaller groupings of threatened Tutsi in this manner.[27] During the first thirteen days of the operation, aside from the camp in Cyangugu, the French reportedly identified only an additional 1,325 "at risk" Rwandans who were moved for their protection. It is not clear how many of these were Tutsi. Over the full course of the operation the French take credit for "evacuating" 3,500 Rwandans, including 1,000 orphans and 600 religious officials, but again it is not clear how many of these were Tutsi.[28]

—They could assemble surviving Rwandans, mainly Hutu, in large camps where Operation Turquoise personnel could protect them more easily and begin to provide humanitarian assistance. In addition, by improving security in the zone, they also enabled humanitarian NGOs to return to Rwanda.

—They could defer the capture of southwestern Rwanda by the RPF and thus forestall an even larger exodus of Hutu refugees into Zaire and Burundi. More than 2 million Rwandans eventually did flee the country, but up to 1.5 million more otherwise might have joined them, which would have caused tens of thousands more deaths from disease in the refugee camps.[29] Ironically, in this way, the intervention probably saved more Hutu lives than Tutsi.

It is impossible to know how many Tutsi still were alive in the SHZ when Operation Turquoise arrived and how many of them perished despite the operation. France estimates that 8,000–10,000 were saved at the stadium in Cyangugu, 1,100 at Bisesero, and about 6,000 in Gikongoro, for a total of 15,000 to 17,000.[30] Several thousand others probably were killed in the zone during the French occupation. French troops also did not intervene to stop looting or to arrest extremists. Lacking the forces, mandate, and interest to serve as a police force, they did not do so. Instead, striving to avoid confrontation and to keep open the possibility of future power-sharing negotiations, the French actually facilitated the safe passage to Zaire of the Hutu government, the army, and the militias, who have contributed to persistent regional instability ever since.

As the army and militias fled to Zaire, Hutu civilians were coerced or chose to flee as well, creating a massive refugee outflow and a humanitarian disaster. In the refugee camps, Hutu army officers and extremists immediately took effective control, refusing to allow fellow Hutu to repatriate and beginning to stage raids back into Rwanda. Not until two years later, when the camps were shelled by the RPA (by this time, Rwanda's army), forcing the armed Hutu elements to retreat hastily deeper into Zaire, did the majority of Hutu civilians return to Rwanda. Many militia members and former army soldiers still remain at bay in the former Zaire (now the Democratic Republic of Congo), from where they spearheaded a major insurgency in northwestern Rwanda in 1997–98. This persistent threat has motivated Rwanda twice (once successfully) to try to overthrow the government of Zaire/Congo, in turn triggering military intervention into that country by states across Africa.[31]

To summarize, Operation Turquoise airlifted some 3,000 troops to neighboring Zaire, of whom about 1,800 crossed the border and created a Safe Humanitarian Zone in southwestern Rwanda. The airlift was expedited by the fact that troops and equipment were already positioned at French bases in Africa. Because the zone encompassed 2,000 square miles and a population of up to 1.5 million Rwandans, the peacekeeping presence was quite sparse. French troops managed to find and protect the single large concentration of Tutsi that still survived in the zone, some 8,000–12,000 at a camp in Cyangugu, as well as a few thousand Tutsi in small groups in outlying areas. However, the peacekeepers failed to protect thousands more Tutsi killed by Hutu during the operation, owing to a French shortage of troops and large transport vehicles and an initial French decision to avoid pockets of killing believed erroneously to consist of two-sided civil war combat. The RPF perceived the French occupation as a hostile attempt to halt their advance and protect Hutu extremists, so the rebels engaged French troops in at least three firefights. However, when French commanders threatened to employ their twelve combat aircraft stationed in Zaire, the rebels acceded to the circumscribed French presence inside the zone. After the operation's two-month mandate expired, the French withdrew in August 1994 and ceded the zone back to the new rebel government and a UN peacekeeping force that remained in Rwanda for another twenty months.

CHAPTER SIX

Transporting

Intervention Forces

If THE UNITED STATES had decided to launch an intervention immediately upon determining that genocide was occurring in Rwanda, a key question would have been how fast an adequate force could have been transported to the theater and begun operations there. Because Rwanda is a landlocked country in central Africa, and because speed is crucial when trying to stop a genocide, the entire force would have had to be airlifted to the theater. To determine how long it would take to deploy such a force to Rwanda, it is useful to look at the experience of past U.S. airborne interventions and the specifics of the Rwanda theater.

Five past U.S. military interventions are especially suitable for analysis because they relied significantly on the rapid airlift of substantial forces: Lebanon (1958); Dominican Republic (1965); Grenada (1983); Panama (1989), and Saudi Arabia (1990). In addition, the U.S. humanitarian operation to aid Rwandan refugees immediately after the genocide—Operation Support Hope—offers key insights about any airlift to the region. Summary statistics for the early airlift portion of the military interventions are displayed in table 6-1. However, only one of the five—the deployment to confront Iraq in 1990, Operation Desert Shield—is analogous to the retrospective Rwanda operation in its long distance to deployment and its being a no-notice operation. The other airlifts were expedited significantly by factors that would have been missing in Rwanda, including: advance notification; a seaport in the theater to enable delivery of bulky equipment by sealift; prepositioning in the theater of U.S. troops, equipment, and logistics; large and convenient theater airfields and staging bases; and most important, short distances from continental American bases to enable frequent sorties by a limited number of airlifters. (For details, see appendix B.)

The most significant statistic in airlift operations is the average daily cargo flow. Personnel are much easier to airlift because they load and unload themselves in a matter of minutes. However, it is imprudent to deploy military personnel into operations without sufficient equipment and logistics. Each planeload of troops requires several planeloads of equipment to support it. Moreover, cargo flights generally require several additional hours on each end to load and unload, which clogs up ramp space and constrains the air flow. Thus the rate of cargo lift effectively constrains the rate of troop deployment.

The airlift for Operation Desert Shield is discussed in some detail here to illustrate the limitations of airborne deployments over large distances. Obviously, the precise composition of troops and equipment for a humanitarian intervention to Rwanda would have differed substantially from that deployed to Saudi Arabia to deter armored aggression by Iraq. However, the constraints on the airlift rate would have been quite similar, making it an appropriate case study.

Other recent interventions by European powers in Africa do not provide appropriate lessons because their deployments were too small or slow for a task like stopping genocide in Rwanda. Moreover, these operations deployed to less violent environments, confronted smaller and less well armed adversaries, and were assisted by larger numbers of local government troops than would have been the case in Rwanda. These differences are best illustrated by examining the two largest such airborne interventions of the past three decades. In May 1978, in the Shaba region of Zaire, 650 French and 1,200 Belgian troops deployed in response to a rebel incursion into the city of Kolwezi. The European forces initiated operations in Zaire within four days of receiving authorization in Brussels, succeeded in evacuating more than 2,000 foreigners in three days, and soon compelled the rebels to retreat. Only eleven European troops, all French, were killed in action. However, this mission was deceptively easy because the rebels numbered a mere 2,500 to 4,500 and were armed only with light weapons and a few heavy machine guns and 81 mm mortars. In Rwanda, by contrast, interveners would have confronted approx-

Table 6-1. *Early Airlift Statistics for Five Previous U.S. Military Interventions*

Destination	Operation	Year	Distance (mi.)	Troops	Early airlift statistics			
					Tons[a]	Days	Troops/day	Tons/day
Lebanon	Blue Bat	1958	2,500	3,234	2,310	6	539	385
Dominican Republic	Power Pack	1965	1,200	16,000	14,000	7	2,286	2,000
Grenada	Urgent Fury	1983	2,000	6,000	n.a.	3	2,000	n.a.
Panama	Just Cause	1989	1,300–3,500	6,157	3,800	7	880	543
Saudi Arabia[b]	Desert Shield	1991	7,000–10,000	2,300	approx. 4,500	9	256	approx. 500

Sources: Roger J. Spiller, "*Not War but Like War*": *The American Intervention in Lebanon*, Leavenworth Paper 3 (Fort Leavenworth, Kan.: U.S. Army Command and General Staff College, January 1981), p. 51; Bruce Palmer, *Intervention in the Caribbean* (Lexington: University Press of Kentucky, 1989), p. 148; Dorothea Cypher, "Urgent Fury: The U.S. Army in Grenada," in Peter M. Dunn and Bruce W. Watson, eds., *American Intervention in Grenada: The Implications of Operation "Urgent Fury"* (Boulder, Colo.: Westview, 1985), p. 99; Robert R. Ropelewski, "Planning, Precision, and Surprise Led to Panama Successes," *Armed Forces Journal International*, February 1990, p. 30.

n.a. Not available.

a. Tons of cargo, not including personnel.

b. Saudi Arabia statistics refer to the ready brigade of the 82d Airborne Division, the first airlifted to the theater.

imately 100,000 soldiers, militia, and rebels, some equipped with armored vehicles, heavy artillery, and surface-to-air missiles. The Shaba interveners also were assisted by 8,000 Zairian army troops in the province, who provided massive superiority in personnel and equipment, thereby eliminating any need for a protracted airlift to the theater.[1] A limited airlift was carried out by eighteen C-141 and one C-5 strategic transport aircraft provided by the United States, four DC-8 and one Boeing-707 aircraft provided by the Europeans, and a dozen Belgian and Zairian C-130 and two French Transall tactical airlifters. To put this modest deployment in perspective, the Belgian forces carried with them only twenty vehicles, mainly jeeps, and no armored personnel carriers or tanks. Viewed in this light, the European intervention in Shaba can be seen as neither major nor decisive. Indeed, as one expert has concluded, "It is probable that the Zairian armed forces would have defeated the rebels even without outside assistance."[2]

The other significant European airborne intervention in Africa in recent times was France's Operation Manta into Chad in August 1983, which was intended to bolster government forces battling Libyan-sponsored rebels in the north. The Manta deployment was fairly substantial, eventually comprising more than 3,000 troops, 700 vehicles, and twenty-seven aircraft. However, this level of force was achieved only gradually because of France's limited airlift capacity, the region's dearth of aviation fuel, and the poor quality of local airfields, which necessitated sealifting and then trucking much of the fuel and equipment along a sea-land route that required four to seven weeks to navigate. During the first week, the French managed to deploy only 818 troops, who lacked any heavy weapons except for 120 mm mortars. Even after three weeks, only 1,750 troops had been deployed. Eight combat aircraft designated for the mission had to be based in foreign countries because of fuel shortages in Chad. After two months, when the mission finally was fully deployed, the combined strength of the small French force and Chad's army still was insufficient to expel the rebels from the country. Eventually, France was compelled to strike a deal with Libya's Moammar Qaddafi that effectively granted him control of the country's north.[3] Like the Shaba intervention, this French deployment in Chad is no model for a successful intervention in Rwanda because it was too slow and too small to have prevented a fast-moving genocide.

Operation Desert Shield

Among previous American airlifts, the deployment to Saudi Arabia in 1990, Operation Desert Shield, most resembles the proposed Rwandan intervention because it demanded an expeditious airlift of large amounts of personnel and equipment over distances up to 10,000 miles and was ordered without advance warning. (Sealift also played an enormous role in Desert Shield but would have been unavailable for a quick deployment to landlocked Rwanda.) The first unit airlifted to Saudi Arabia was the ready brigade of the 82d Airborne Division, comprising about 4,500 tons of equipment and 2,300 personnel and requiring 165 sorties. After one day's preparation, loading out the brigade from Fort Bragg and Pope Air Force Base consumed seven days, considerably longer than the army expected. The constraining factor was not the number of aircraft available but the unit's ability to generate cargo, which took so long that some airlifters originally designated for loading at the base were diverted to other missions.[4] The brigade did not close in Saudi Arabia until nine days after receiving its orders, an average airlift of only 500 tons of cargo and 250 troops per day.

Subsequently, when several continental U.S. bases began to load out simultaneously and several Saudi airfields were utilized, the rate of airlift increased dramatically. During the first month, the workhorses of dedicated strategic airlift—a team of 110 C-5 Galaxy and 234 C-141 Starlifter aircraft—carried 41,500 tons of cargo and nearly 39,000 personnel, averaging approximately 1,400 tons and 1,300 personnel per day.[5] Still, total airlift rates were well below planning assumptions. The nominal capacity of U.S. strategic airlift was some 48.5 million ton miles per day (MTM/D), while actual airlift in the first month was only eleven MTM/D, or 23 percent of capacity.[6]

This subpar airlift performance in Desert Shield has been attributed to several factors, many of which likely would have recurred if President Clinton had ordered a large-scale military airlift to Rwanda. These include: the lack of a staging base for pilots in the theater, which meant that more pilots had to be aboard each round trip to the theater to relieve each other, in turn leading to a shortage of flight crews; limited ramp space at bases en route; lower than expected aircraft payload capacity (60–88 percent of that projected) and utilization rates (50–67 percent of that projected); the late call-up of reserve pilots; and repeated last-minute planning changes, which played havoc with on-load rates. These factors compounded each other. For example, the only aircraft suitable for outsize cargo, the C-5, took an average of three days to make the round trip from the United States to Saudi Arabia and had a low 68 percent availability rate. Thus, although 110 C-5 aircraft had been dedicated to the airlift, only about twenty-five per day were available for loading, and each held approximately 15 percent less than anticipated.[7] As a result, though the C-5 fleet theoretically had the capacity to hold 7,800 tons of cargo, only about 1,500 tons per day could be loaded aboard them at peak efficiency.

Operation Support Hope

Airlifting U.S. troops to Rwanda would have been considerably slower even than Desert Shield owing to several factors—longer distances, more constrained air refueling, scarcer theater fuel supplies, and smaller theater airfield capacity. The best evidence for this is Operation Support Hope, the U.S. humanitarian airlift ordered by President Clinton immediately after the end of the Rwandan genocide, on July 22, 1994. The airlift was intended to improve conditions in refugee camps in eastern Zaire and thereby avert the death by disease of hundreds of thousands of Rwandan Hutu who had sought refuge there. It traced the same route and utilized the same airfields—Entebbe, Uganda; Goma, Zaire; and Kigali, Rwanda—as likely would have been used had the United States earlier launched an intervention to stop the genocide.[8] Although the airlift for Operation Support Hope was much smaller than would have been required for a full-blown military intervention, it nevertheless strained the resources of Central Africa and the U.S. Air Force.

For this belated humanitarian intervention, most strategic airlifters were loaded in the United States, had to be refueled over the Atlantic by U.S.- or U.K.-based tankers, landed for servicing and refueling in Spain, and then had to refuel again in the "Greek corridor" over the Mediterranean to reach central Africa.[9] Nonstop flights from the United States to the theater were possible but were rare because of limitations on assets such as airborne refueling.[10] Airlifters originating in Europe refueled once in Germany and then again in the Greek corridor. At first, most strategic sorties landed at Uganda's Entebbe airport, approximately 200 miles from Rwanda, because the United States had not yet recognized the RPF's new government. At Entebbe, cargo was transloaded onto smaller, tactical C-130 aircraft for the last leg to Goma. Only a few strategic flights went directly to Goma because the airfield's capacity was small and its runway inferior. After Washington recognized the new Rwandan government in late July, the airlift was gradually shifted to Kigali airport, which by late August was receiving the bulk of strategic sorties.[11]

Because fuel was limited or nonexistent at Entebbe, Goma, and Kigali, many aircraft were forced to refuel in Kenya on their return. However, the Kenyan airfields of Mombasa and Nairobi also ran out of fuel initially. Some assistance was provided by four KC-10 tankers, which ferried fuel from Zimbabwe to Entebbe and conducted airborne refueling above Goma.[12] Still, the airlift's fuel demand threatened to disrupt commercial aviation across Africa until Shell International was contracted to fill the gap. The U.S. Air Force deployed teams to ten bases around the world to coordinate the airlift. Other assets—such as tankers, airlifters, and flight crews—were stretched thin because of a simultaneous humanitarian airlift operation in Bosnia.[13]

Constraints on Airlifting a Force to Stop the Genocide

These previous experiences indicate that the limiting constraint on the rate of airlift for a counterfactual military intervention to stop the Rwandan genocide would have been one of four factors: the initial load-out at continental U.S. bases; airborne refueling in the Greek corridor; airfield capacity in the theater; or refueling capacity in the theater. By contrast, the capacity of the U.S. airlift fleet would *not* have been a significant constraint on the intervention unless another major operation had been under way simultaneously. In 1994 the workhorses of dedicated strategic airlift for the U.S. armed forces would have been approximately the same as those used in Desert Shield less than four years earlier: 234 C-141 aircraft and 110 C-5 aircraft. In general, the average number of airlifters available per day for loading depends on the round-trip time to the theater and the percentage of aircraft undergoing maintenance. For example, given a four-day round trip to central Africa, an average of one-fourth of total aircraft could be loaded daily. Maintenance requirements reduce this number by perhaps another third, leaving one-sixth of the fleet available each day for loading, or approximately thirty-nine C-141 and eighteen C-5 aircraft.

The nominal payload of an airlifter is a function mainly of two variables: the distance of its maximum leg between refuelings, and whether it is operating in a wartime environment when limits are increased by up to 30 percent. During Desert Storm, the maximum leg was approximately 3,500 miles, which yields a nominal wartime payload of twenty-six tons for the C-141 and approximately seventy-two tons for the C-5. In practice, however, the average payloads carried by these aircraft were nineteen and sixty-one tons, respectively. The calculations that follow employ rounded estimates of twenty and sixty tons. In theory, if weight were the only constraint, payloads could be increased considerably by relying more on airborne refueling. However, in practice, volume rather than weight of cargo is often the limiting factor; in logistics parlance, aircraft "cube out" before they "gross out." As a result, twenty and sixty tons are realistic average payloads for the two types of aircraft even with somewhat shorter distances between refueling.[14] Thus the daily capacity of the dedicated strategic airlift fleet of C-141 and C-5 aircraft for an intervention in Rwanda in 1994 would have been approximately (39 x 20 tons) +

(18 x 60 tons), or more than 1,800 tons per day, not a significant constraint in relation to the factors discussed next.

Load-Out

In Desert Shield, the ready brigade of the 82d Airborne Division—working as quickly as possible—required seven days to load out 2,300 personnel and approximately 4,500 tons of cargo on 165 sorties. Even slower was the initial task force of the 101st Air Assault Division, which was built around its ready brigade and consisted of 2,742 personnel and approximately 4,000 tons of cargo, including 117 helicopters. Ordered to deploy on August 9, 1990, the force was not ready for loading until August 14 and did not "close" in the theater—the military term for the completion of a unit's arrival—until August 31, a full three weeks after the order.[15] Discounting for initial preparatory work, the daily load-out rate was 600 tons for the 82d, which was loading out as quickly as possible, and less than 300 tons for the 101st, which may have been constrained by availability of airlifters. There is no reason to believe that constraints on load-out had been relieved between 1990 and 1994. Indeed, the first rigorous study of the delays encountered during the load-out in Desert Shield was not published until 1993.[16] Accordingly, 600 tons per day appears to be the maximum realistic load-out rate for forces drawn from a single U.S. airborne division at one base in 1994.

Greek Corridor

After refueling in Europe, airlifters would have had to refuel again over the Mediterranean to reach central Africa. However, owing to international air space constraints and the time required for airborne refueling, in "the Greek corridor . . . a maximum of 24 airlift missions per day could flow through the air refueling track."[17] Depending on the mix of C-141 and C-5 aircraft employed, this Greek corridor bottleneck would have limited daily flow to between 480 and 1,440 tons. (These estimates are based on the average aircraft payloads experienced in Desert Shield, which were some 15–25 percent below nominal wartime levels.)[18]

Airlifts in the 1980s and early 1990s commonly employed a mix of aircraft that included two of the smaller but more plentiful C-141s for every one of the larger but more scarce C-5s. Assuming that mix of the two airlifters and the average payloads identified earlier, the daily maximum capacity through the Greek corridor would have been 800 tons (sixteen C-141 aircraft, each holding twenty tons, plus eight C-5 aircraft, each holding sixty tons).[19] In

Operation Support Hope, however, only enough tankers were deployed to support nine C-141 and five C-5 missions through the corridor daily, partly because of the simultaneous demand for tankers to support no-fly-zone and humanitarian relief operations in Bosnia, according to the commander of the humanitarian intervention in Rwanda and the army's "After Action Report" for the Rwandan relief effort. This smaller deployment of air tankers constrained realistic throughput via the Greek corridor for Operation Support Hope to 480 tons daily.[20]

Theater Airfield Capacity

Airfield capacity is extremely difficult to pinpoint in the abstract because it depends on so many manipulable variables, as laid out in a recent analysis by the Rand Corporation:

> It depends on the usability of different areas of the airfield for parking different types of aircraft, on the changing mix of cargoes the aircraft carry (and, hence, the times needed to on-load or off-load), on the distances from the previous airfield and to the next airfield (and, hence, the fuel needed), on whether transiting aircraft make quick stops or need extended ground time (e.g., for crew rest), on whether the airfield operates with peacetime levels of manning and equipment or is augmented with additional resources, and on many other factors.[21]

Nevertheless, the experience of regional airfields during Operation Support Hope is instructive and enables an estimation of the realistic daily throughput capacity of each airfield. These capacities could have been attained only gradually, of course, as airfield operations were optimized at theater facilities unaccustomed to such large air flows. (For details on airfield utilization in Operation Support Hope and how the following estimates of maximum daily airfield capacity were derived, see Appendix C.)

In a maximum intervention, the main theater airfield almost certainly would have been Kigali, with a daily capacity of 400 tons. The main staging base would have been Entebbe, also with a capacity of 400 tons. Cargo arriving at Entebbe would have been transloaded to tactical aircraft for sorties to Kigali and Rwanda's smaller airfields, or otherwise unloaded and trucked to Rwanda. (UNAMIR deputy commander Anyidoho reports that the land route from Entebbe to Kigali—via Kampala, Kagitumba, and Rwamagana—was good and required only a ten-hour drive. Indeed, this route was used by the UN during the genocide, because Kigali airport was closed, to resupply UNAMIR, then to evacuate it, and eventually to redeploy troops for UNAMIR

II. The UN also used helicopter flights from Entebbe to the Rwandan border, though not all the way to Kigali.)[22] Strategic airlifters carrying helicopters also could have been unloaded at Entebbe, from where the rotary aircraft could have self-deployed to Rwanda. Goma and some of the area's smaller airstrips probably would have been used, but almost exclusively for tactical sorties from Entebbe and Kigali. Thus maximum capacity for strategic airlift to Rwanda, once the region's main airfields had been upgraded, would have been about 800 tons daily.

Fuel Supply in the Theater

During Operation Support Hope, "fuel was undoubtedly the greatest issue facing Tactical Air Coordination Center (TACC) planners," according to the army's after-action report.[23] With virtually no fuel at theater airfields, arriving airlifters had to carry sufficient fuel reserves to permit them, after unloading cargo, to fly to a foreign airport to refuel. The main such refueling stop was Mombasa, Kenya, which could be resupplied by sea; it operated seventeen hours daily, and had ramp space for five C-141 and two C-5 aircraft simultaneously. Assuming maximum payloads and canonical turnaround times, this pit stop had sufficient refueling capacity for "812 tons of C-141 and 700 tons of C-5 cargo," or 1,512 tons of total daily throughput.[24] However, this theoretical capacity is extremely sensitive to real-world perturbations. Assuming payloads were 20 percent lower and turnaround times 20 percent higher than planned, as in Desert Shield, Mombasa's throughput would be only 1,000 tons. If turnaround times were double canonical estimates, as occurred at some airports in Desert Shield, maximum daily throughput would be only 600 tons.[25]

Any one of these four constraints on the rate of airlift could have proved most limiting during a deployment to stop the genocide, depending on the operational decisions that were made. For example, if the intervention force comprised a single organic airborne division, as the 1965 Dominican Republic operation did, the limiting factor would have been load-out. Neither the 82d nor 101st Divisions can load out more than about 600 tons daily. In theory, this rate could triple if three brigades from different divisions were loaded out simultaneously; but this would have required the entire U.S. dedicated airlift fleet at the time, which was unrealistic given U.S. obligations in Bosnia and elsewhere.[26] In any case, other constraints would not have permitted such a high rate of airlift. Kigali and Entebbe airports could absorb only a combined total of about 800 tons daily. Air refueling in the Greek corridor likewise was limited to about 800 tons, assuming a realistic mix of aircraft, and might have been as low as 500 tons if there were competing demand for airborne refueling tankers. Finally, refueling at Mombasa could have presented the greatest constraint if average payload and turnaround times were substantially lower than canonical estimates.

Each of these constraints could have been alleviated somewhat by ingenuity and commitment of resources. For example, the rate at which the theater could accept strategic airlift could have been increased by also utilizing the airport at Bujumbura, Burundi, from which cargo could have been trucked to Rwanda, less than a 100-mile drive away. (This land route was fairly reliable and was used in reverse to evacuate Americans from Kigali to Bujumbura during the first few days of the genocide.) The Greek corridor's cargo throughput could have been increased by raising the percentage of bigger C-5s in the air flow. Theater fuel demands could have been alleviated by establishing a staging base in Jeddah, Saudi Arabia, from which round trips to central Africa do not require refueling. (The Jeddah option was rejected in Operation Support Hope, apparently because Saudi permission was required.)[27] Alternatively, Mombasa's airfield could have been converted to twenty-four-hour operations, increasing its theoretical refueling capacity by 40 percent. Helicopters also could have self-deployed from Europe or from marine vessels off the African coast, freeing up some cargo space on strategic airlifters.[28]

In practice, however, military logistics are never optimized, and as a result, airlift rates never approach canonical estimates. For the U.S. Armed Forces, as demonstrated by the five previous full-blown airborne interventions outlined in table 6-1, this is true even for high-priority airlifts to confront identified, imminent threats to vital national security interests. It strains credibility to assume, as one previous analyst has, that the United States would deploy more efficiently to address humanitarian concerns than it has to secure vital national interests in the past.[29] If anything, it is likely that humanitarian interventions would be conducted with comparatively less efficiency than traditional interventions because they are deemed of lower priority by both military and political officials. Moreover, the previous analyst's reliance on canonical estimates of airlift capacity, rather than empirical evidence from previous airlifts, makes his assumptions about potential deployment rates unrealistically optimistic. In light of the real-world constraints on airlift discussed in this chapter, it turns out to be much harder to "save lives with force" than previously has been asserted. Indeed, in a realistic deployment to Rwanda in 1994, at least one of the four constraining factors likely would have limited airlift to no more than 800 tons daily. Accordingly, that level of throughput is taken as the maximum credible rate for the remainder of this study.

CHAPTER SEVEN

Plausible

Interventions

HAD THE UNITED STATES acted immediately upon determining that genocide was occurring, it could have launched a military
intervention some two months before France's eventual Operation Turquoise.
This chapter analyzes the retrospective potential of three types of U.S. military
intervention: maximum, moderate, and minimal. None envisions full-blown
nationwide policing or long-term nation building by American troops. Long-
term deployment of American troops to a region of little intrinsic national
interest would have been neither strategically necessary nor politically feasible.
After the acute genocidal situation was relieved, the mission would have been
handed off to a multinational force, presumably under UN authorization.
Details of such a follow-on mission would have been crucially important, but
they are beyond the scope of this study.

Full-blown policing is ruled out because the force requirements would
have been excessive. James T. Quinlivan has analyzed historical data from such
policing operations and concluded that "the size of stabilizing forces is determined by the size of the population and the level of protection or control that
must be provided within the state."[1] In situations of moderate unrest, such as
ongoing turmoil in India's Punjab state or the 1965 U.S. intervention in the
Dominican Republic, force ratios of "four to ten per thousand of population"

are needed, including both military and police. In situations of greater unrest, such as the 1952 Malayan Emergency, ratios of ten to twenty per thousand of population are required. Policing Rwanda during the genocide certainly would have required the higher force density. Given Rwanda's 1994 population of about 8 million, the force requirement would have been 80,000–160,000 troops. That is far more than would have been feasible politically or logistically, considering that it represents 10 to 20 percent of all active duty U.S. soldiers and marines and a much higher percentage of the combat troops among them. However, it is important to emphasize that Quinlivan's study focuses on full-blown policing operations. By contrast, operations merely to secure an area and prevent large-scale violence require a smaller presence. On the low extreme, France's Operation Turquoise was able to employ a density of less than 1.5 troops per thousand of population in the Safe Humanitarian Zone because it deployed after most Tutsi had been killed.

Though full-blown policing was not a realistic option in Rwanda, several other intervention scenarios can be envisioned. These alternatives can be distinguished by the extent of their goals and the degree of cost and risk they would entail. Maximum intervention would have used all feasible force to halt large-scale killing and military conflict throughout Rwanda. Moderate intervention would have sought to halt some large-scale killing but without deploying troops to areas of ongoing civil war, in order to reduce U.S. casualties. Minimal intervention would have relied on air power, avoiding any introduction of U.S. ground troops into Rwanda.

Maximum Intervention

A maximum intervention would have required deployment of a force roughly the size of a U.S. division—three brigades and supporting units, comprising about 15,000 troops. The rules of engagement would have permitted deadly force to protect the lives of endangered Rwandans. After entering and establishing a base of operations at Kigali airport, the force would have focused on three primary goals: (1) halting armed combat and interposing between FAR and RPF forces on the two main fronts of the civil war in Kigali and Ruhengeri; (2) establishing order in the capital; and (3) fanning out to halt large-scale genocidal killing in the countryside. None of these tasks would have been especially difficult or dangerous for properly configured and supported U.S. troops once in Rwanda. However, transporting a force of appropriate size 10,000 miles to a landlocked country with limited airfield capacity is not a trivial exercise, and would have taken considerably longer than some retrospective appraisals have suggested. For example, one unrealistic estimate is that of Iqbal Riza, deputy to the director of UN peacekeeping during the genocide and later chief of staff to UN Secretary General Kofi Annan. Riza has asserted that—given the requisite will—sufficient troops and tanks to stop the genocide could have been airlifted to Rwanda in two days.[2] As will be shown later in this chapter, his estimate is low by at least a factor of ten.

The first brigade to arrive would have been responsible for Kigali—coercing the FAR and RPF to halt hostilities, interposing between them, and policing the capital. The second brigade could have deployed one of its battalions north to halt the civil war in Ruhengeri, another as a rapid-reaction force in case U.S. troops drew fire, and a third to begin stopping large-scale genocide outside Kigali. The third brigade would have been devoted entirely to halting killing in the countryside.[3] Military personnel requirements for such an effort would have been roughly 2,000 to halt war in Kigali, 1,000 to halt war in the north, 3,000 to police Kigali, 1,500 for a rapid-reaction force, and 6,000 to stop the genocide in the countryside, in addition to perhaps 1,500 support personnel for peace operations, making a total of about 15,000 troops. The 3,000 troops to police Kigali would have represented a ratio of at least ten per thousand of population in the capital.[4]

To stop a genocide that was occurring mainly in the countryside, helicopters would have been optimal for reconnaissance and rapid reaction, especially for areas far from major roadways. The utility of helicopters for such a countergenocide operation was also emphasized by a special panel of the Carnegie Commission on Preventing Deadly Conflict that examined the retrospective potential for intervention in Rwanda: "Reconnaissance, command and liaison, transport, and attack helicopters would be very useful for gathering information, providing responsive and precise fire support, and enabling the force to achieve a significant advantage in mobility over belligerents."[5] However, these low-flying and slow aircraft are particularly vulnerable to surface-to-air missiles, anti-aircraft artillery, and even small-arms fire—a serious concern given that President Habyarimana's plane had just been shot down—which probably would have constrained how helicopters were deployed in Rwanda.

Among U.S. Army divisions, the 101st Air Assault has by far the largest number of helicopters, approximately 380, which is three times the number in the 82d Airborne and four times the number in a standard light division. However, deploying the entire 101st Division to Rwanda would have been excessive and would have deprived the United States of its premier air assault assets for other contingencies. More appropriate would have been a task force comprising one brigade each from the 101st, the 82d, and a light division, reinforced with ground transportation assets and additional company-size units useful in peace operations. These extra units would have included medical, intelligence, communications, civil-military operations, and psychological operations companies. The communications companies would have included some language interpreters, although these would have come mainly from the local population, as they do in most humanitarian operations. Recent trends also suggest that U.S. Marines probably would have been included in the operation, despite the long distance from any littoral; for example, one army brigade could have been replaced by a Marine Air Contingency Force (ACF)—their version of a ready, rapid-reaction unit—reinforced with a regimental combat team, extra helicopters, and motorized vehicles.[6]

Because Rwanda is a landlocked country in central Africa, and because of the premium on speed when trying to stop a genocide, the entire division-size task force would have been airlifted to the theater. Owing to constraints on the rate of airlift, as discussed earlier, the time required to deploy the intervention force would have been a function of its weight. Estimates of the weight and other characteristics of a division-size task force built around one brigade each from the 101st, the 82d, and a light division can be taken as the average of those divisions—26,550 tons, including 200 helicopters and 13,373 personnel.[7] In practice, the task force would have attached additional motorized vehicles and support units essential to peace operations and left behind some organic heavy weapons intended for combat operations; however, the net effect on weight would not have been significant.[8] At the maximum credible rate of 800 tons daily, such a task force would have required thirty-three days of airlift. Several additional days must be allotted for the delay between the deployment order and starting the airlift—in Desert Shield, this was less than two days for the 82d Division and eight days for the 101st Division—plus several days more for the gradual ramp-up of capacity at theater airfields and for aircraft to travel to the theater and be unloaded. In addition, the rate of force deployment might have been inhibited over time by the need to use limited airlift capacity for food, medicine, spare parts, and other logistics to sustain the first arriving echelons. Thus the entire force could not have closed in the theater until about forty days after the president's order.

However, lead elements would have begun operations much sooner. Approximately four days after the order, a battalion or two of army rangers would have parachuted in and seized Kigali airport at night.[9] Follow-on troops would have expanded this airhead to establish a secure operating base. Within another week, sufficient U.S. forces would have arrived—on the order of 5,000 troops and 3,000 tons of equipment—to dispatch battalions to halt fighting and interpose between the FAR and RPA in Kigali and northwestern Rwanda. While one or both sides in the civil war might have tested the interveners, a display of firepower likely would have deterred further challenges, just as during Operation Turquoise the French threat of escalation after a few firefights was sufficient to deter RPA incursions into the safe humanitarian zone. By about two weeks after the deployment order, sufficient troops and equipment would have arrived to fully police Kigali.

Only subsequently, as sufficient helicopters, vehicles, and troops arrived, could the intervention force have turned in earnest to stopping the genocide in the countryside. The task force's personnel could have been front-loaded in the first few days of the airlift, but they would not have ventured far into the countryside until a secure operating environment had been ensured in Kigali and the northwest and until sufficient transportation assets and equipment had arrived. An analogy is provided by the case of the initial brigade of the 82d Airborne Division to be deployed in Desert Shield. In that case the brigade's first battalion began operations in the theater on August 13, 1990, six days after receiving its deployment order, but it undertook only the relatively low-risk activity of securing the port of Jubail. Mechanized forces and helicopters did not even begin arriving until the next day. As a result, the brigade did not deploy into the desert until August 23, 1990, some sixteen days after its deployment order.[10] In Rwanda, the delay before deploying into the field would have been even longer because of the distance and difficulty of the airlift. Thus U.S. troops would not have begun stopping genocide in the countryside until about three weeks after the president's order, or May 11, 1994.

Optimists such as Human Rights Watch have suggested that genocide would have stopped spontaneously throughout Rwanda upon arrival of a Western intervention force in Kigali—or possibly even earlier upon the mere announcement of a deployment. They also assert that "because the operation of the genocide was highly centralized, stopping the killing in Kigali would have quickly quelled violence elsewhere in the country."[11] This is dubious. Genocide was in full swing throughout Rwanda by the time President Clinton had enough information to reasonably issue an order on April 20, 1994. To stop the killing everywhere at once would have required the extremist ringleaders to issue clear and direct orders over the radio and through military channels to cease and desist. There is little reason to believe they would have done so spontaneously because they did not do so during Operation Turquoise, even after their French allies urged them to halt the killing.

Some optimists argue that the extremists would have halted the killing in hopes of avoiding punishment. However, these Hutu already were guilty of genocide and had no reason to believe that stopping midway would gain them absolution. Perhaps if intervention had been combined with explicit international offers of immunity from prosecution and political asylum for extremist Hutu leaders willing to call off the genocide, such orders might have been issued. But the international community never offered, or even considered offering, such a deal at the time. Indeed, most supporters of humanitarian intervention are human rights advocates who on principle would be unalterably opposed to offering immunity or asylum to perpetrators of genocide, even if doing so might reduce violence in the near term.

More likely, the announcement of Western intervention would have accelerated the killing as extremists tried to finish the job and eliminate witnesses while they had a chance. Such was the trend ahead of the RPA advance, as militias attempted to wipe out remaining Tutsi before the rebels arrived.[12] (A similar pattern was observed in Kosovo in 1999, as NATO's bombing of Yugoslavia apparently triggered a substantial acceleration in ethnic cleansing by Serb forces against Albanians in the province.) During the Rwandan genocide, the ringleaders even trumpeted false reports of impending Western intervention to help motivate Hutu to complete the killing.[13]

The only plausible way for late-arriving interveners to have stopped the genocide without deploying to the countryside would have been to capture the ringleaders and force them to issue the appropriate orders. This mission would have been difficult because the extremist leaders retreated to Gitarama on April 13, ten days before American forces realistically could have arrived in Kigali. Even had the ringleaders been captured and so coerced, genocide might not have stopped immediately in the countryside, especially if the rebels had continued their offensive, which terrified the Hutu populace and motivated the Hutu militias to try to finish off the remaining Tutsi civilians, who were seen as natural allies of the advancing rebels.

The 6,000 U.S. troops deployed to the countryside would have been insufficient to establish a full police presence but could have found and protected significant concentrations of threatened Rwandans. Smaller-scale killing of isolated Tutsi in the countryside probably would have continued for several days or weeks after the arrival of interveners because of a shortage of motorized vehicles and ground troops, just as occurred in areas captured by the RPA and in the French-occupied zone of Operation Turquoise. However, if the Pentagon had consulted with any regional experts as part of its intelligence preparation of the battlefield (IPB), the intervention force would have known to look for large groups of Tutsi congregated at central sites. Not only had Rwandans fled to such sites during previous explosions of ethnic violence, but UNAMIR reported in the weeks before the genocide that some Rwandans were seeking refuge at UN and church sites and that some asylum centers had been established.[14] Helicopter reconnaissance could have identified large assemblages of Rwandans from the air. U.S. troops then could have been deployed quickly, ideally by helicopter, to disperse hostile forces, secure the sites, and hand them off to military police and civil affairs units. In some cases, ironically, the troops would have discovered that they had rescued Hutu from revenge-seeking Tutsi rebels, because such retaliatory attacks would have been indistinguishable from the anti-Tutsi genocide when reconnoitered from the air.

The number of troops required to guard each site would have varied but been relatively small, in light of the weakness of armed opposition and the high quality of U.S. personnel, communications, and rapid response. For smaller gatherings of a few hundred up to a few thousand, a platoon could have stood guard initially and then escorted the displaced persons to a larger camp. Centralization in larger camps would have reduced countrywide guard requirements, facilitated the provision of emergency humanitarian aid, and enabled the subsequent hand-off of displaced persons to UN peacekeepers and NGO relief agencies responsible for resettlement.[15] Approximately twenty large sites might have been established, each holding at least 10,000 Rwandans guarded by approximately 150 troops, including military police, civil affairs personnel, and a combat platoon. Once the threatened Rwandans were so concentrated, force requirements at the camps would have been only about 3,000 troops, including twenty combat platoons—approximately the size of a single combat brigade.

Aerial reconnaissance could have relied on about forty helicopters, or 20 percent of the task force's total. Fuel would have been air-tankered to Kigali, then lifted to tactical refueling points by cargo helicopters using fuel bladders.[16] Assuming that three-fourths of this reconnaissance fleet had been on the ground at any one time—as is typical to permit crews to rest and other personnel to perform routine maintenance—approximately ten helicopters could have been kept aloft round the clock. Given Rwanda's total area of about 10,000 square miles, and assuming a conservative average ground speed of seventy-five miles per hour and a conservative search radius of one mile, an exhaustive search of the country could have been conducted in less than seven hours.[17] Such reconnaissance units could not have peered through dense jungle or inside buildings where smaller groups were held but could have found the large groups being held in cleared areas such as stadiums, athletic fields, ranches, and courtyards.

In practice, search patrols probably would have been interrupted when groups of threatened or hostile Rwandans were found, in order to summon and direct response forces. Assuming 100 such sites were found, each causing a three-hour interruption, 300 helicopter search-hours would have been lost, delaying completion by thirty hours. The entire country thus could have been covered in about thirty-seven hours of searching. In other words, assuming good weather and sufficient fuel, only about three days of daylight searching would have been required to identify most large concentrations of threatened Rwandans. The search would have been delayed somewhat if it confronted air-craft losses, fuel shortages, or bad weather. On the other hand, the search could have been expedited somewhat by searching at night, which would have been possible using certain modern army helicopters equipped to fly at night. (Older helicopters such as the Cobra, Huey, and Kiowa A/C are not equipped for night operations; the Kiowa also is incapable of flying at more than 4,000 feet above sea level, making it inappropriate for much of Rwanda, which has a high elevation.) Employing night-vision goggles, helicopter patrols could have identified large groups of displaced Rwandans by their concentration of cooking fires. (Ironically, extremist Hutu killers on the ground sometimes used those same cooking fires to locate hidden Tutsi.) Ground troops would have been deployed to the biggest and most threatened sites as they were found, and to the others soon after.[18]

Such a dedicated search for threatened civilians would have been very effi-cient but somewhat unorthodox in a combat environment. If instead the U.S. ground commander insisted that helicopters serve a more traditional recon-naissance role, probing just ahead of ground troops as they radiated out from Kigali, the search would not have been completed until infantry units reached Rwanda's borders by ground. This type of methodical ground advance would have been slowest through Rwanda's densely populated west and south and might have required two weeks to complete.

Thus, depending upon the search method, large-scale genocide could have been stopped during the fourth or fifth week after the deployment order, or sometime between May 15 and May 25. Interestingly, that would have been before the task force even closed in the theater, because its supporting equip-ment and logistics still would have been arriving for another week or two. However, it is not unusual for combat operations to be expedited in this man-ner; indeed military planners often differentiate between the initial "Alpha echelon" of an airlift, which consists of the fighting force, and the "Bravo echelon," which includes supporting equipment and logistics.[19] According to the model of the genocide's progression discussed in Chapter 3, and assuming the Hutu extremists neither accelerated nor decelerated their rate of killing appreciably when the intervention was announced, such an intervention would have enabled about 275,000 Tutsi to survive the genocide, as compared with the 150,000 who actually did. Maximum credible intervention thus could not have "prevented" the genocide, as some have claimed, but could have spared about 125,000 Tutsi from death, some 25 percent of the genocide's ultimate toll.

Moderate Intervention

A more modest intervention designed to reduce force requirements and the risk of casualties would have refrained from deploying U.S. troops to any area in Rwanda in which FAR and RPA troops were actively engaged in combat. In late April 1994, this approach would have confined U.S. troops to a zone consisting of six prefectures in southern and western Rwanda that were still free of two-sided military combat but already consumed in genocide—Butare, Cyangugu, Gikongoro, Gisenyi, Gitarama, and Kibuye. Such an intervention would have been similar to France's Operation Turquoise but would have been implemented sooner and covered a larger area.[20] A single reinforced brigade would have sufficed, given that the territory, population, specific tasks, and potential adversaries would not have been as great as those envisioned in the maximum intervention. Ideally, the ready brigade of the 101st Air Assault Division would have been designated, supplemented by two additional light infantry battalions, support units for peace operations, and additional helicopters and motorized vehicles—for a force of 6,000 personnel, weighing about 10,000 tons (see figure 7-1).

Three main objectives would have been set: (1) to deter and prevent entry of organized military forces into the zone; (2) to halt large-scale genocide there; and (3) to prepare for a hand-off to a UN force. By the time of intervention, the zone would have included about 4 million residents.[21] Six thousand troops would have represented about 1.5 per thousand of population in the zone, too low for policing but roughly equivalent to the presence in Operation Turquoise.[22] Strategic airlift would not have relied on Kigali airport, which was still a battleground in the civil war, but on Bujumbura, Burundi, from which cargo could have been transported to western Rwanda by truck, helicopter, or fixed-wing tactical airlift. Entebbe would have been a stage to receive additional strategic airlift sorties and to transload cargo for tactical sorties to Bujumbura or the smaller airfields in the western half of

Figure 7-1. *Zone of Hypothetical Moderate Intervention*

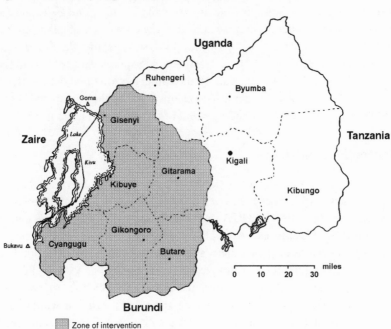

Rwanda and neighboring eastern Zaire. Airlift probably would have been most constrained by load-out from the United States, because the 101st Division can generate at most 600 tons of cargo daily. At that rate, seventeen days would have been required for loading out the force. Several additional days must be allotted for the delay between the intervention order and the start of load-out, the gradual ramp-up of theater airfield capacity, travel time to the theater, and unloading. Accordingly, the force could not have closed in the theater until more than three weeks after the deployment order.

The first goal of arriving troops would have been to secure the zone's perimeter—to deter, detect, and repel military incursions. Primarily, this would have required monitoring the eastern border of the zone, about seventy miles long abutting Kigali and Ruhengeri prefectures. Given the relative weakness of potential infiltrators—whether FAR soldiers or RPA rebels—this initial mission might have been accomplished by frequent helicopter patrols of the border, if necessary calling on rapid-reaction airborne troops to respond to any detected incursions. A reinforced airborne battalion would have been sufficient to carry out this reconnaissance mission and could have been airlifted to the theater first, within about a week of the deployment order. Deployment of this vanguard could even have been expedited somewhat by assigning the mission to the 1-508th Airborne Battalion Combat Team, the U.S. Army's only airborne battalion based in Europe.[23]

Within another week, sufficient troops and equipment would have arrived to begin to stop genocide. The 101st ready brigade contains seventy-three organic helicopters and ideally would have been reinforced with additional rotary aircraft to ensure that twenty could be dedicated to the search for threatened Tutsi. By employing half the number of helicopters as the maximum intervention to cover less than half the territory, an exhaustive daylight search again could have been completed in about three days, assuming good weather and sufficient fuel. Large-scale genocide in the zone probably could have been stopped within three weeks after the deployment order, or by May 11, 1994. The model of the genocide's progression suggests that about 200,000 Tutsi within this zone could have been kept alive by such an intervention, about twice the 100,000 who actually did survive in this portion of Rwanda. Elsewhere in Rwanda, genocide would have continued until stopped by the RPA, as actually occurred; no additional Tutsi would have been spared by the intervention outside the zone besides those who actually did survive the genocide in any case. Moderate intervention thus could have spared about 100,000 Tutsi from death, or 20 percent of the genocide's ultimate toll. Interestingly, moderate intervention would have saved almost as many lives as maximum intervention in Rwanda, for two reasons. First, by avoiding combat areas and thus the need to establish a cease-fire, a moderate intervention could have turned more quickly to stopping the genocide. Second, a moderate intervention would have been aimed at the southern and western regions of Rwanda because of the absence of civil war combat there in April and May 1994, but these regions also coincidentally possessed high concentrations of Tutsi.

Minimal Intervention

To further reduce the risk of casualties, a minimal intervention would have attempted to mitigate the genocide without introducing U.S. ground troops into Rwanda. Instead it would have relied on air power from bases in neighboring countries. In light of the current perceived American aversion to casualties, this type of low-risk intervention can serve as an alternative to deploying ground troops or doing nothing. Three air power strategies were possible in Rwanda:

Coercion

The United States could have threatened to bomb the extremist ringleaders and the FAR's military assets until genocide was halted. If the threat alone initially failed to coerce them, subsequent U.S. bombing would have served the dual purpose of further coercing Hutu leaders and providing a form of air support to the RPA, which was stemming the genocide as it advanced. One potential shortcoming of this strategy is that if the threat alone had failed to stem the killing, U.S. airmen would have had difficulty locating the ringleaders. The United States has failed in three recent attempts to target foreign political leaders from the air: Libya's Moammar Qaddafi in 1986, Iraq's Saddam Hussein in 1991, and Yugoslavia's Slobodan Milosevic in 1999. In addition, Rwandan government troops would have been difficult to distinguish from rebels in areas where they fought in close quarters. For example, during three months of fighting in Kigali, Presidential Guard and RPF troops were separated by only 100 meters. The difficulty of precise bombing in such conditions was demonstrated in Kosovo in 1999, when NATO air strikes against Serb troop formations near the end of the campaign also inadvertently killed many Kosovo Liberation Army (KLA) fighters.[24] However, the experience of European powers in postcolonial Africa demonstrates that the deployment of limited air power can have a dramatic impact in the short term.[25] If air coercion had achieved such near-term success in Rwanda, a follow-on ground force almost certainly would have been required to sustain the peace.

Airborne Policing

Rather than coerce leaders, airborne policing would have attempted to interdict physically and intimidate psychologically the actual perpetrators of the genocide throughout Rwanda. Significant numbers of U.S. attack helicopters and possibly fixed-wing aircraft would have patrolled Rwanda daily from bases in neighboring countries. If armed factions were spotted threatening large groups of civilians, air-to-ground fire would have been used to disperse the assailants at least temporarily. Such patrols would have continued until the deployment of a non-American peace enforcement mission or until the RPA won the civil war.

Safe Passage

A third strategy would have been to facilitate the escape of Tutsi from Rwanda to refugee camps in bordering states—Burundi, Tanzania, Uganda, and Zaire—by using helicopter patrols to ensure free passage on Rwanda's main exit routes. These patrols would have been a variant of a more traditional military mission in which air cavalry units are "used to conduct security patrolling and main supply route security missions . . . to keep the enemy from massing and possibly provide early warning of larger enemy movements."[26] Interestingly, establishing such camps in Zaire, Tanzania, and Burundi was actually Washington's preferred option during the second month of the genocide in May 1994, but this concept was not embraced by the United Nations and in any case did not include any plan to help Tutsi reach the border.[27] Had safe passage been pursued seriously, U.S. ground troops would have deployed to one or more neighboring states to establish and initially protect the camps. U.S. helicopters could have operated from staging bases established at Bujumbura or Goma, both of which are near Rwanda and have airfields capable of receiving air tankers carrying helicopter fuel. To reduce transit distances to eastern Rwanda, additional bases might have been established nearby across the border; these bases could have been supplied with fuel by cargo helicopters carrying fuel bladders.

Signal and psychological operations units, employing radio broadcasts and leaflets, would have directed Rwanda's Tutsi to use the exit routes. Radio signals can be broadcast from specially equipped C-130 aircraft, known as Commando Solo, operated by the 193d Special Operations Group of the Pennsylvania Air National Guard. They can broadcast AM, FM, shortwave, and TV audio signals and have been employed in interventions in Grenada, Panama, the Persian Gulf, Somalia, and Haiti. In Serbia in 1999 they broadcast ten-kilowatt AM and TV signals, and a one-kilowatt FM radio signal "equivalent to the strength of a medium sized American station." Rwanda is sufficiently small that the entire country could have been penetrated by signals at various times of the day if such aircraft had circulated around the perimeter of the country. It is likely that at least Uganda, Burundi, and Tanzania would have granted permission for such use of their airspace.[28]

Rwanda has only about 600 miles of paved roads.[29] Assuming a team of twenty helicopters, of which one-fourth (five helicopters) could have been kept aloft at one time, each would have been responsible for only 120 miles of roadway. At a ground speed of 120 miles per hour, each section of roadway could have been patrolled hourly, on average.[30] Air-to-ground fire could have been used to break up roadblocks and disperse armed gangs to facilitate the free flow of refugees. This mission could have been extended to Rwanda's unpaved main roads, but doing so would have multiplied fivefold, to 3,000 miles, the length of roadway to be covered and resulted in less frequent and thus less effective patrols. Another 5,000 miles of unpaved tertiary roads could

Table 7-1. *Projected Outcome of Three Plausible Interventions*

Extent of intervention	Force size	Duration of airlift	Tutsi saved	Percentage of genocide's toll
Maximum	Division 15,000 troops 27,000 tons	40 days	125,000	25
Moderate	Reinforced brigade 6,000 troops 10,000 tons	21 days	100,000	20
Minimal	Air assault brigade 2,500 troops (outside Rwanda) 4,500 tons	14 days	75,000	15

Source: Author's calculations.

not have been patrolled without spreading resources so thin that the overall effectiveness of the operation would have been undermined.

The ready brigade of the 101st Division could have handled any of these air-power strategies, especially if supplemented by strike aircraft as necessary. The brigade weighs about 4,500 tons, including some 2,500 troops. Loading out this smaller force would have required only about eight days. However, adding several days to account for the typical initial delay following the deployment order, transit to the theater, gradual ramp-up of theater airfield capacity, and unloading, the brigade would not have closed in the theater until about two weeks after the deployment order, or May 4. Use of air power in the theater could have begun as soon as sufficient helicopters and fuel had arrived, most likely in late April.

Each of the air power strategies would have had drawbacks. Coercion might not have worked because of the difficulty of finding and targeting extremists and their military assets. Airborne policing would have been only a stopgap measure, dependent on cobbling together a follow-on ground force and unable to prevent smaller acts of genocide in the meantime. Facilitating safe passage would have protected only those Rwandan Tutsi able to make their way to major exit routes, left many others to die, and created refugee crises in neighboring states. U.S. helicopters also would have been vulnerable to anti-aircraft fire, and any resulting casualties could have undercut American public support for the mission.

Nevertheless, each of the air power options also had the potential to save tens of thousands of Rwandan Tutsi from demise. Coercion might have stopped the genocide quickly and thereby paved the way for a cease-fire in the civil war. Airborne policing could have protected some threatened Tutsi long enough to be saved by France's Operation Turquoise or a similar follow-on deployment. Facilitating free passage likewise would have kept more Tutsi alive, albeit as refugees, and they might have returned home quickly upon the RPA's victory in the civil war. Based on the model of the genocide's progression, about 300,000 Rwandan Tutsi were still alive in late April 1994, of whom about 150,000 subsequently perished. If minimal intervention had been able to avert half these later killings, it could have spared about 75,000 Tutsi from death, or 15 percent of the genocide's ultimate toll (see table 7-1).

CHAPTER EIGHT

Contending
Claims

MANY CRITICS OF WESTERN inaction in Rwanda have claimed that timely intervention would have prevented the genocide. Some even originally asserted that UNAMIR could have done so by itself, had it merely been ordered to do so. However, it is now acknowledged that the UN peacekeepers were inadequately equipped for such a mission. For example, Astri Suhrke, coeditor of a multinational study on the response to the Rwandan genocide, has testified that even "if UNAMIR had stayed, it wouldn't have influenced the situation because it lacked everything. It had neither more munitions, nor provisions, nor even sandbags." Likewise, Alison Des Forges of Human Rights Watch has withdrawn her earlier claims, testifying: "General Dallaire has convinced me that it would have been dangerous for UNAMIR to go on the attack if it had been alone."[1] Nevertheless, such commentators still hold that a few thousand well-armed reinforcements would have been sufficient to avert the killing.

For this reason, the West's failure to prevent Rwanda's genocide is generally attributed exclusively to a lack of will. A former Clinton administration official, for example, blames the failure to stop the genocide on the fact that "there was no pre-determined foreign policy goal of halting genocide when feasible."[2] Likewise, human rights activists have urged the United States to adopt an explicit policy of intervening to prevent genocide, on the grounds that if such a policy had existed in 1994 the Rwandan genocide would never have occurred.[3] Such assertions rarely if ever have been subjected to rigorous scrutiny. Six prominent variations are so analyzed in the text that follows. Interestingly, many of them were enunciated first during the genocide and have been repeated ever since by the same proponents, unaffected by subsequent evidence.

Diplomatic Intervention

The boldest claim is that of Alison Des Forges, who contends that mere diplomatic intervention could have averted the genocide without additional military deployment:

> Rwanda depended heavily on foreign financial support. . . . Any public condemnation of the genocide by the combined donors and the World Bank, particularly if accompanied by an explicit warning that they would never fund a genocidal government, would have shown Rwandans that the interim government was unlikely to succeed and made them less likely to implement its orders. . . . Perhaps those completely committed to exterminating Tutsi would have continued that course. But they had been few at the start and they would have found it more difficult to recruit others—or to retain their loyalty—once it was clear that the interim government could not succeed in the international arena."[4]

According to Des Forges, upon the outbreak of violence in April 1994, if the international community had threatened to halt aid to any Rwandan government that committed genocide, Hutu moderates would have been emboldened to face down the extremists and extinguish violence. As evidence, she cites two main points: moderate FAR officers appealed for support to Western embassies during the first days of violence,[5] and the intensity of massacres and propaganda waned after the West increased its condemnations in late April 1994. She argues that if the FAR moderates had publicly declared their opposition to genocide, the Rwandan populace quickly would have followed suit, and the little-respected extremist leader, Colonel Théoneste Bagosora, probably would have backed down and called it off. Bagosora was weak-willed and could have been deterred, she claims, citing as evidence that he abandoned his original plan for an explicit military coup in response to opposition from colleagues and UN officials in Rwanda. If Bagosora had nevertheless resisted, she further contends, the FAR moderates could have joined forces with the RPF to defeat the extremists militarily.[6]

Although Des Forges is an expert on Rwanda and the genocide, her claims here are dubious. The most relevant fact is that virtually all of Rwanda's elite military units were controlled by extremist Hutu, who were led by Colonel Bagosora, a retired army colonel who held the post of acting defense minister on the day President Juvenal Habyarimana was killed. In the hours and days after the assassination, Bagosora apparently orchestrated both the genocide and the formation of the extremist interim government to support it. As Belgian scholar Filip Reyntjens observes: "Bagosora's power during this period derived from control of several key units of the army (the Presidential Guard, the reconnaissance battalion, and the paracommando battalion), with which he could act outside of ordinary military channels."[7] These 1,500 to 2,000 elite troops were equipped with armored vehicles and represented the cream of Rwanda's armed forces, as attested by UNAMIR's deputy commander, Henry Anyidoho: "In contrast to the [regular army], the Presidential Guards were well looked after and properly equipped. In effect, two separate standards were maintained in the army.... The Presidential Guard were viewed as soldiers of the elite regiment, whereas the majority of the regular forces were ignored." Providing further evidence of the relatively poor quality of the regular army, during the first days of renewed civil war in April 1994 thousands of FAR troops were unable to defeat the single RPF battalion that they surrounded in Kigali. In some cases, even the irregular militias were more potent than elements of the regular army, perhaps owing to better morale. For example, the most prominent militia, the Interahamwe, "established a series of roadblocks at which they intimidated the regular Rwandan government forces even though they were like allies to the government forces." The extremists, who controlled not only the militia but all of the army's elite forces, vividly demonstrated their power and ruthlessness by killing Rwanda's top political moderates during the first two days of violence.[8]

By contrast, moderate Hutu officers had virtually no effective troops at their disposal. This faction included General Augustin Ndindiliyimana, Colonels Marcel Gatsinzi and Léonidas Rusatira, and Lieutenant Colonel Ephrem Rwabalinda. Gatsinzi was nominally army chief of staff for ten days immediately after the assassination, until replaced with an extremist on April 17, but he commanded no troops. Rusatira was head of the military school and had no troops under his command. Ndindiliyimana commanded about 1,000 relatively weak national police, who had neither combat training nor heavy weapons and were kept in defensive positions after the outbreak of violence.[9] Thus the moderates avoided challenging the extremists, not because of a lack of Western rhetorical support but because of mortal fear for themselves and their families. Indeed, a leading Hutu moderate officer confessed to this author that the reason he did not confront the extremists forcefully was because his entire extended family lived in the countryside and would have been killed in retaliation.[10] This fear was justified given the behavior of the extremists at the time. Throughout the genocide they stamped out any nascent opposition— coercing and bribing moderate politicians, removing them from office or killing them if they did not yield, shipping moderate soldiers to the battlefront, and ordering civilian opponents of genocide to be killed as "accomplices" of the rebels.[11]

Des Forges herself notes that nominal chains of command were meaningless in a situation where extremists controlled the power. The orders issued by extremist subordinates prevailed over those of moderate superiors. For example, on April 10, 1994, the moderate army chief of staff, Colonel Gatsinzi, ordered subordinates to stop killing civilians, but was completely ignored. Similarly, in Kibungo the prefect opposed the genocide but was unable to prevent it from starting on April 7, even though he was not removed from office until two weeks later.[12]

Realistically, the most that could be expected of the moderates was for them to stay neutral and try to broker a peace, which they did despite a lack of encouragement from Western officials. Some observers have cast a harsher judgment, accusing the moderates of "cowardice" and "passive complicity."[13] It is true that some officers known as "moderates" because they pursued peace were actually motivated not by opposition to genocide but by the stark realization that the Tutsi rebels would soon win the civil war unless it were stopped. Regardless of the reasons, however, FAR moderates did seek Western assistance and did try to broker peace with the RPF during the early days of the genocide. For example, on April 7, during a long phone conversation, Ndindiliyimana asked the Belgian ambassador for assistance in composing a moderate group of military officers to press for peace. Rusatira also had contacts with Belgian, U.S., and French officials. On April 12 he drafted a letter urging a truce and a halt to the killing of innocents, which was signed by ten moderate FAR officers and broadcast over the radio. In response, the extremists threatened him with death, forcing him into hiding. From April 16 to April 22, Rusatira again tried repeatedly to persuade officials of the government, political parties, and radio stations to call off the killing and embrace his proposed cease-fire. However, even the rebels rejected the cease-fire offers on grounds that the genocide was continuing and that the moderates were powerless to rein in the extremists. As one Rwandan journalist has noted, it was not that the moderates were complicit but that they "sadly had no influence." Even

Des Forges concedes that "Bagosora's clear superiority in arms and troop strength" was a key reason the moderates failed to challenge the extremists forcefully.[14]

Interestingly, Des Forges originally enunciated her belief in the power of international condemnation during the first month of the genocide, stating: "The international community must immediately and unanimously declare that any government established upon a hundred thousand bodies will never receive any form of international recognition or assistance. Such a statement must be widely diffused by radio within Rwanda to encourage moderates within the army to resist the murderous massacres being carried out by extremists."[15] Perhaps in response to such urging, Western officials did transmit warnings to Rwanda's military and political leaders through private channels, which were soon publicized by the two leading moderate FAR officers in an attempt to rein in their more extremist colleagues. On April 22 the moderate officers Rusatira and Ndindiliyimana called for a halt to killing on grounds that the genocide "could discredit Rwanda with foreign governments whose support was essential."[16] However, the extremist interim government was unswayed by these warnings two weeks into the genocide, and there is no reason to believe such warnings would have been any more effective if they had been made earlier or more publicly.

Des Forges correctly notes that there was a decline in massacres in late April 1994, but this decline can be explained most simply by the dwindling number of Tutsi who remained alive in Rwanda at that point.[17] Evidence for this straightforward interpretation is the fact that mass killing of Tutsi continued a little longer, through early May, in Butare—one of only two prefectures where large numbers of Tutsi still remained alive because the genocide had started late and the prefecture's original Tutsi population was large. International condemnation did little but compel extremists to disguise their rhetoric and try harder to hide the killing—for example, by taking Tutsi away from public roadblocks before killing them. It did not significantly impede the genocide.[18]

Incendiary rhetoric did decrease, but it did not disappear. For example, Radio-Television Libre des Mille Collines (RTLM) continued through late April to call for all remaining Tutsi in Kigali to be killed by May 5. In addition, many of the reported calls to reduce violence were directed not at anti-Tutsi ethnic killing but at Hutu-on-Hutu criminal and political killing, which exploded as societal norms against murder were abandoned to implement the genocide. Explicit appeals for Hutu to be sure to kill only "the enemy"—that is, Tutsi—began as early as April 12, 1994, and were expanded in response to growing anarchy later that month. There were also some public calls for a halt to violence against Tutsi, but many of these were ruses to lure Tutsi out of hiding in order to kill them. Moreover, Des Forges concedes that vitriolic rhetoric and killing resurged in mid-May, just as the United Nations demonstrated renewed outrage at the violence by authorizing the redeployment of peacekeepers in UNAMIR II, which appears to contradict her theory of the restraining power of international condemnation. Ironically, the extremists' few gestures toward moderation were directed mainly at persuading France to renew its military support for the anti-Tutsi war—hardly an indication of sincere moderation.[19]

Even if Des Forges were right in her assumption that early explicit economic threats would have compelled the Rwandan government to halt violence and offer peace, the RPF might not have accepted. Having agreed to a cease-fire in February 1993, only to be rewarded by genocide, the rebels now were intent on victory and quite confident they could accomplish it on their own. It is possible that only robust foreign military intervention could have compelled the Tutsi rebels to accept a cease-fire.

Finally, Des Forges raises the possibility that with Western encouragement the FAR's moderate Hutu officers could have joined forces with the Tutsi rebels to defeat the rest of the Hutu army and militias. This was feasible militarily given that the Tutsi rebels by themselves ultimately defeated the entire Hutu army and militias in just three months. However, it was implausible politically. By the time of the genocide, Rwanda had been severely polarized along Hutu-Tutsi lines by four years of civil war, the calculated efforts of propagandists, the RPF advance toward Kigali in February 1993, and the October 1993 massacre of Hutu by Tutsi in neighboring Burundi. Even moderate Hutu politicians once allied with the rebels had come to fear Tutsi hegemony.[20] Though the moderate Hutu officers sincerely pursued a cease-fire and halt to the genocide, they could not conceivably have defected to the Tutsi rebels, at least until the defeat of the FAR became imminent. Even Des Forges concedes that "with the resumption of the war and the ensuing pressure for solidarity, officers opposed to Bagosora found it increasingly difficult to challenge his actions." As early as April 8, just two days after Habyarimana's assassination, the erstwhile moderate officers acceded to the new extremist interim government: "With the RPF pushing ahead vigorously, they felt pressure to shun politics and devote themselves completely to the work of being soldiers."[21]

Only when the FAR was on the brink of total defeat did the moderates emerge again. On July 6, 1994, after the RPF had captured Kigali and Butare and the genocide was all but over, two leading FAR moderates, Gatsinzi and Rusatira, finally denounced the interim government and announced they were committed to fighting the genocide. Even then, however, they did so only from the security of the French-occupied zone, at Kigeme. After the RPF won the war, the victorious rebels rewarded these two defeated moderate Hutu officers by incorporating them into the new Rwandan army.

Five Thousand Troops Prevent Genocide

The most common claim is that 5,000 troops deployed soon after the outbreak of violence could have prevented the genocide. The claim is generally associated with UNAMIR Commander Dallaire, who reportedly requested such a reinforcement on April 10, 1994, in a telephone conversation with UN headquarters in New York. He hoped to make a show of force with guns and tanks that he believed would deter further violence in Kigali: "Dallaire believed that 5,000 troops would be enough to prevent the terror from spreading." A subsequent May 1, 1994, version of the Dallaire plan reportedly called for 1,800 troops to be airlifted directly into Kigali, and another 3,200 to enter Rwanda on the ground from Uganda in the north. Only about 500 of UNAMIR's original force would have remained in Rwanda, resulting in a total troop level of about 5,500. On May 6, 1994, a resolution authorizing this troop level was presented in the UN Security Council by the nonpermanent members, and on May 17 UNAMIR II was authorized, but implementation was so slow that the troops arrived after the genocide was over. Dallaire has bemoaned the missed opportunity ever since. More recently, an expert panel of military officials with experience in peacekeeping, assembled by the Carnegie Commission on Preventing Deadly Conflict, has endorsed Dallaire's claim, differing only on a few specifics.[22]

However, the basic claim is problematic on three grounds. First, both Dallaire and the Carnegie Commission panel apparently assume the intervention force would have arrived almost immediately upon being ordered to deploy. The Carnegie report states that the 101st Division's ready brigade "is able to establish itself in a 24-hour period over a distance of about 450 miles," which may be accurate for deploying the first echelon of the brigade over a short distance but is irrelevant for deploying the entire brigade more than 10,000 miles. The report also provides no indication that in 1991 the same brigade needed three weeks to deploy to Saudi Arabia. The report does observe that the airlift would require "approximately 90–100 strategic aircraft sorties," which is plausible with a high proportion of C-5s in the mix, but it gives no indication of the protracted time needed to load this many lifters or the limited capacity of Kigali and Entebbe to handle such an air flow.[23]

In reality, the required airlift would have been protracted. Dallaire had requested some 5,000 high-quality, fully equipped reinforcements because he planned to retain only about 500 of UNAMIR's best troops for the mission. Even if Dallaire had retained his entire 2,500-man UNAMIR force of uneven quality and requested only 2,500 reinforcements, the airlift still would have taken much longer than he or the Carnegie report suggests. A U.S. light infantry ready brigade—which contains about 2,500 personnel and weighs about 2,500 tons—would have required about a week from a no-notice order to begin any significant operations in the theater, and several more days for all its equipment to arrive.[24] Further delays would have resulted if the brigade were reinforced with heavy armor or helicopters, the respective preferences of Dallaire and the Carnegie Commission. For purposes of comparison, a mechanized division weighs six times as much, and an air assault division twice as much, as a light division.[25] Still more time would have been required to assemble a multinational force as Dallaire envisioned. Thus, even if the UN had urgently heeded Dallaire's April 10 request, reinforcements probably could not have begun serious efforts to stop the genocide before April 20, by which time half the ultimate victims of the genocide already were dead. This calculus also shows that even if the U.S. government had paid more attention to the early evidence of mass killing obtained by the DIA, it could not have intervened quickly enough to prevent the genocide.[26]

Moreover, it is unrealistic to argue that an urgent intervention should have been launched on April 10, when most of the international community did not even realize genocide was being attempted until at least ten days later. Indeed, to argue that the United States should have deployed combat forces to Rwanda before senior officials even suspeced that genocide was occurring is to argue that such deployments should be a commonplace response to civil war. That standard would have required enforcement operations during the past decade in Albania, Algeria, Angola, Azerbaijan (Nagorno-Karabakh), Bosnia, Cambodia, Congo Republic, Croatia, Ethiopia, Kosovo, Liberia, Sierra Leone, Somalia, Sudan, Tajikistan, and Zaire, some on several occasions. Obviously, such a policy is unsustainable. It is deceptive to argue that Rwanda was a special case deserving immediate attention, because that did not become clear until two weeks later.

Second, both Dallaire and the Carnegie Commission mischaracterize the progression of the genocide, claiming it was confined to Kigali for the first two weeks, only later spreading outward. According to Carnegie, there was a "window of opportunity . . . from about April 7 to April 21, 1994" during which intervention "could have stemmed the violence in and around the capital [and] prevented its spread to the countryside ... throw[ing] a wet blanket over an emerging fire."[27] In reality, killing started in most areas of Rwanda by April 7 or 8,[28] peaked a week later, and by April 21—the last day of the purported "window" for preventive intervention—half the ultimate Tutsi victims were already dead. Even had reinforcements arrived overnight in Kigali, Dallaire was unaware at the time that genocide was being perpetrated outside the capital and so would not have known to deploy troops to the countryside in time to prevent the massacres.

It is understandable that Dallaire could have misconstrued the progression of the genocide in April 1994; from his bunker in Kigali, where he spent most of his time trying to arrange a cease-fire, he had limited access to information from the countryside. However, it is inexplicable that neither he nor the Carnegie Commission availed themselves in the intervening years of available historical information to revise their assessments. In April 1997, after viewing a draft of the Carnegie Commission report more than a year before its publication, this author informed the lead writer of the draft that he had incorrectly characterized the genocide's progression, but the error was not corrected in the final report. Instead, a footnote was added stating: "Scholars, observers, and practitioners have differing views on the rate of the spread of violence in the Rwandan situation and the width of any intervention 'window.' But even those who have reservations about how much time was available to intervene do not reject the existence of a window of opportunity for action."[29] Though true, this last sentence fails to note that the window of opportunity was narrower than the time required for deployment. In other words, it would have been physically impossible to deploy Carnegie's recommended intervention force during the actual window of opportunity—a fact that undermines virtually all of the report's conclusions.

Third, 5,000 troops would have been insufficient to stop genocide without unacceptable risks of failure or casualties. This is especially true of Dallaire's original plan, which called for 2,000 troops to be airlifted to Kigali, the rest to enter on the ground from the north, and none to deploy immediately to the south and west of Rwanda, where most Tutsi lived and were being exterminated rapidly, unbeknownst to Dallaire. The Carnegie Commission's plan, devised in retrospect, is superior. It recognizes the need to airlift the entire force to Kigali, utilize a helicopter-heavy force like the 101st ready brigade for transportation and rapid response, and stop all major violence. Its three missions are identical to those proposed in chapter 8 of this book for a maximum intervention: stop the civil war, restore order in Kigali, and prevent killing in the countryside. However, the need to stop genocide in the countryside did not become clear until about April 20, 1994, so it is unrealistic to argue that an earlier deployment should have been tasked with this mission from the outset.[30]

Under any plan limited to 5,000 troops, only about 1,000 likely would have been available for policing Kigali—some three per thousand of population, which is grossly inadequate for a city in the throes of genocide. In the countryside, U.S. commanders would have had a terrible choice: they could either have concentrated forces for effective action, leaving most of the country consumed in genocide, or they could have spread forces thin, leaving troops vulnerable to attack. The Carnegie Commission report argues that a small contingent could have succeeded in part because of the "shock" value of airborne forces. However, this suggests compellence rather than enforcement, a point that the report indirectly acknowledges by stating that any "delays in achieving political stability would require higher force requirements over time."[31]

Thus the Carnegie report quietly concedes that 5,000 troops would have offered only a hope rather than any strong assurance of success. In the real world, U.S. military planners insist on deploying sufficient troops to ensure the success of an intervention—24,000 for the Dominican Republic, 22,500 for Panama, and 21,000 for Haiti, all countries with populations smaller than Rwanda's. The planned force for Haiti in September 1994 is especially illustrative because that country was an equally or less challenging target for intervention than Rwanda in virtually all respects. Haiti had an area about the same, a population only 80 percent as big, a much smaller army of 7,000, a comparably sized militia of 20,000–30,000, and much lower levels of violence than Rwanda. Yet the U.S. commander assembled a "formidable force of nearly 21,000 soldiers, sailors, airmen, marines, and coast-guardsmen."[32] Given this American doctrine of sizing forces adequately to ensure success, when Belgium floated the proposal of a small reinforcement of UNAMIR's 2,500 troops before the genocide, U.S. military officials were opposed on grounds that such a force would still be too small to stop real conflict. Indeed, Dallaire himself declared six weeks *before* the genocide in Rwanda: "If I wanted to guarantee safety I would need 40,000 troops here."[33]

UN Response to the "Genocide Fax"

According to many critics, UN headquarters had three months' advance notice of genocide and could have averted it simply by authorizing raids on weapons caches as had been requested by its field commander. First reported in 1995, the story has reemerged perennially in the media as a purportedly new exposé. These critics cite the so-called "genocide fax," a January 11, 1994, cable from General Dallaire to UN headquarters in New York.[34] The cable conveyed an informant's warning that extremists were planning to provoke renewed civil war, kill Belgian peacekeepers to spur their withdrawal, and slaughter Tutsi using a 1,700-man Interahamwe militia that the informant was training in Kigali: "He has been ordered to register all Tutsi in Kigali. He suspects it is for their extermination. Example he gave was that in twenty minutes his personnel could kill up to 1,000 Tutsis."[35] The informant also reported an arms cache containing "at least 135 weapons," which Dallaire wanted to seize within thirty-six hours. Three days later, the United Nations refused permission for the raid and directed Dallaire first to seek confirmation of the accusations from President Habyarimana.[36] When Dallaire did so, the plotters were tipped off, and they quickly distributed the weapons. Critics claim that if the United Nations had acted responsibly Dallaire could have seized the weapons and derailed the genocide plot.

This argument is flawed both in criticizing the UN's decision and in assuming a rosy scenario had it acted otherwise. Prudence dictated seeking confirmation of such an extreme accusation before authorizing action. Indeed, Dallaire's own cable had expressed doubt about the informant's credibility, stating: "Force Commander does have certain reservations on the suddenness of the change of heart of the informant . . . Possibility of a trap not fully excluded, as this may be a set-up." Interestingly, all major press reports on the genocide fax engage in selective quotation, failing to cite this key passage that reflects Dallaire's own skepticism about his warning.[37] Raising further doubt, the cable was the first and only from Dallaire containing such accusations. During civil wars, warnings of coups and assassinations often prove to be erroneous, so that it is essential to confirm any new accusation before taking action.[38] Then-UN Secretary General Boutros Boutros-Ghali has explained that "alarming reports from the field . . . are not uncommon within the context of peacekeeping operations." Likewise, Iqbal Riza, deputy to the director of UN peacekeeping during the genocide, explains that "in the heat of the moment" it is hard to differentiate authentic warnings because "we get hyperbole in many reports."[39]

Directing Dallaire to discuss the allegations with Habyarimana was especially appropriate given the informant's belief that "the president does not have full control over all elements of his old party/faction." Boutros-Ghali also sent a demarche to Habyarimana on January 13, 1994, directing him to take corrective action within forty-eight hours and warning that failure to do so would force the UN to make the accusations public and to take appropriate measures. When it became clear that Habyarimana was not cooperating, UN headquarters granted conditional authorization for weapons raids three weeks later, on February 4, and Boutros-Ghali took Dallaire's accusations to the Security Council on February 10, 1994, two months before the genocide.[40] The council responded with a statement on February 17, 1994, warning both sides in Rwanda of "the consequences for them of non-compliance" with "their obligation to respect the weapon-free zone established in and around the city [Kigali]." The council also implied that these consequences would be withdrawal of UN forces, stating that "UNAMIR will be assured of consistent support only if the parties implement the Arusha Peace Agreement fully and rapidly."[41] Apparently, the council hoped to compel Habyarimana's compliance by threatening to withdraw its peacekeepers and thereby leave his regime vulnerable to attack by the RPF rebels. The Rwandan president was plausibly susceptible to such threats because he no longer enjoyed the protection of French troops, which had withdrawn in December 1993 following the arrival of UN forces.

Also rarely noted is the fact that Dallaire never reported back to the UN that he had found any confirmation of the plot before the genocide. UN official Shaharyar M. Khan testified in 1998 that he had conducted a review of all of the correspondence to New York from both Dallaire and the secretary general's special representative in Rwanda before Habyarimana's death and "found no reference" to planning for genocide except the single cable from Dallaire: "In UNAMIR reports and assessments, there is frequent mention of re-arming, of military confrontation, of high ethnic tension and of a descent towards civil war but no reference to a planned and systematic killing of the civilian population."[42]

Adding further grounds for caution at the UN was Belgium's warning that its peacekeepers were unable, under their existing mandate, to take effective action against the extremist militias. Accordingly, Boutros-Ghali was afraid of provoking an escalation and transforming UNAMIR's mission into "peacemaking instead of peacekeeping," as a Belgian cable noted at the time.[43] The dangers of peacemaking—formally known as "peace enforcement"—had been underscored only a few months earlier by the deaths of American troops in Somalia.

Even if the United Nations had acquiesced to Dallaire in January 1994, it is unlikely the weapons cache could have been seized or that doing so would have prevented the genocide. UN headquarters actually did reverse itself barely three weeks later, on February 4, 1994, granting Dallaire authorization to raid weapons depots in accordance with UNAMIR's existing mandate and rules. However, his forces failed in every such attempt, even after an informant identified three new caches on February 7. By mid-March, the peacekeepers had captured a total of sixteen weapons and 100 grenades.[44]

The real obstacles to seizing weapons were UNAMIR's limited mandate, rules of engagement, equipment, and personnel. Under its Chapter VI mandate, the peacekeeping force served at the pleasure of the government of Rwanda. The UN Security Council had authorized the peacekeepers "to contribute to the security of the city of Kigali *inter alia* within a weapons-secure area established by the parties," but the rules of engagement—which had been approved by both the Rwandan army and the rebels—required that any raids be conducted in cooperation with national and local police.[45] Belgian peacekeepers actually tried this several times, but as investigators later concluded, "these operations couldn't be effective at all, because of the ties that united the Rwandan national police with the extremist Hutu militias."[46] Furthermore, UNAMIR was not equipped or trained to face any serious opposition. Armored personnel carriers did not begin arriving until late February, so peacekeepers would have been vulnerable to small-arms fire at the time Dallaire originally requested his raid. As Dallaire later conceded, even UNAMIR's "Quick Reaction Force" was not "trained, equipped, nor operationally to be prepared to conduct any offensive assault operations."[47]

Several anecdotes provide further evidence that UNAMIR's failure to seize weapons resulted from inadequate forces, training, and equipment, rather than from the UN's delay in authorizing offensive actions in response to the genocide fax. On February 6, 1994, two days after receiving authorization from UN headquarters for weapons raids, UNAMIR ceased searching for weapons at checkpoints because the searches were leading to confrontations with Rwandan soldiers. A month later, Bengali colonel Shamsul Mowla complained, "We know where the arms depots are but we are told that we can't go in and get them" because of the lack of training and equipment. On April 7, 1994, the day after Habyarimana's plane was shot down, Dallaire decided not to rescue ten Belgian peacekeepers held by extremists at an army base because his troops and equipment were inadequate for such an offensive operation; this inaction resulted in the deaths of the Belgians. Also on April 7, the reliability of Bengali troops was called into question. Bunkered in a stadium, they were too scared even to open the gate to permit the entry of Belgian peacekeepers who were being pursued by Rwandan soldiers and militia; the Belgians were forced to scale a fence to gain refuge.[48]

Furthermore, if the United Nations had permitted Dallaire to act without consulting local authorities, Kigali could have responded by simply expelling the force, whose presence in Rwanda was subject to the consent of the host nation, as with all consensual UN peacekeeping operations. The peacekeepers also were vulnerable to violent retaliation because they were dispersed rather than consolidated in defensible locations.[49] Moreover, Dallaire's cable identified a cache of only 135 arms, whereas the government had imported at least 20,000 rifles and 500,000 machetes over the preceding two years for distribution to the army and militias.[50] Even if Dallaire had managed to seize this tiny cache without prompting expulsion or retaliation, he could not possibly have derailed the wider genocide plot without significant reinforcements.

Silence the Hate Radio

Because radio stations helped incite and direct the killing, some observers have argued that quickly jamming or destroying their transmitters upon the outbreak of violence could have averted the genocide. A Belgian peacekeeper who monitored broadcasts testified, "I am convinced that, if we had managed to liquidate RTLM [Radio-Télévision Libre des Mille Collines], we could perhaps have avoided, or in any case limited, the genocide." A human rights advocate characterizes jamming as "the one action that, in retrospect, might have done the most to save Rwandan lives."[51]

Such claims are specious, because radio broadcasts were not essential to perpetuating or directing the killing. By April 1994, Rwandans had been sharply polarized along Hutu-Tutsi lines by civil war, propaganda, and recent massacres in Burundi. The assassination of President Habyarimana and the allegation of Tutsi responsibility was sufficient trigger for many extremist Hutu to begin killing. Moderate Hutu were not usually swayed by radio broadcasts, but rather by threats and physical intimidation from extremist authorities. Moreover, orchestration of the genocide relied not merely on radio broadcasts but on the government's separate military communications network. Indeed, the broadcast range of the radio transmitter of the infamous RTLM was limited to greater Kigali. (Radio Rwanda, which "was not as racist as RTLM," had a transmitter able to broadcast nationwide.) Belgium's military staff apparently considered attacking RTLM soon after the outbreak of violence; they requested the coordinates of the transmitter site on April 7 and received them from UNAMIR the following day, but then demurred. A week later, on April 16–17, 1994, the RPF actually did destroy the RTLM transmitter, but the station soon resumed broadcasting, apparently from Radio Rwanda's transmitter, so that the attack perversely increased the broadcast range of the hate radio station. The temporary silencing of RTLM failed to inhibit the genocide in any way. It also did not prevent the genocide from spreading to Rwanda's final two prefectures in the days immediately following.[52]

Ironically, silencing the radio might have had more impact before the genocide, when broadcasts were fostering polarization, but such action would have been rejected at the time as a violation of sovereignty. Indeed, after the genocide came to light and the State Department's political-military adviser for the region proposed jamming the radio transmissions or broadcasting counter-programming, a Pentagon lawyer still claimed that any such action would violate the American principle of freedom of speech, and the proposal was rejected. Even if hate radio had been extinguished preventively, however, the extremists possessed and used other means to foster hatred, including "the press, education, religious training, [and] the discourse in sections of the [ruling party]," according to Jean-Pierre Chrétien, an expert on Rwanda's hate machine. As Chrétien concludes, "radio is not the only determinant of public opinion. . . . [T]he Rwandan population had a lot of trouble resisting an ethnic opposition constantly on the scene."[53]

Evacuators as Interveners

Belgian scholar Filip Reyntjens argues that the Western forces that were sent to evacuate foreign nationals during the first week of violence could have restored order in Kigali and thereby averted the genocide, if only they had been given additional orders. Reyntjens urged this course publicly on April 9, 1994, as quoted in *Le Soir*, April 11, 1994. He warned that if the French, Belgian, and U.S. troops being deployed "only evacuate their nationals, it will lead directly to a catastrophe. . . . It is necessary to neutralize the Rwandan army in Kigali." Belgium's foreign minister, Willy Claes, simultaneously pursued this strategy with UN Secretary General Boutros-Ghali in a meeting in Bonn, hoping to modify UNAMIR's mandate to permit such an operation. According to Claes, "Paris said no resolutely, and the Americans wouldn't even consider it." France apparently had little interest in a military confrontation with the RPF, and the United States was still applying the lessons of Somalia. After Claes was rebuffed in this search for support, he notified the secretary general on April 12 that Belgium would be withdrawing its UNAMIR contingent. Looking back, UN commander Dallaire asserts that the strategy proposed by Reyntjens "could easily have stopped the massacres." Likewise, a senior French military official, General Christian Quesnot, subsequently testified that 2,000 to 2,500 determined soldiers "could have stopped the massacres launched in Kigali."[54]

(Interestingly, neither officer appears to offer an estimate of the casualties expected from such a mission.)

Reyntjens reports that on April 10, 1994, just four days after Habyarimana's assassination, some 1,400 lightly armed Western troops, mainly Belgian and French, were already in Kigali. The newly arrived evacuators included 450 from Belgium, 450 from France, and 80 from Italy, who complemented Belgium's 410-man contingent in UNAMIR. In addition, 1,100 reserves were less than two hours away from Kigali by air; Belgium deployed a reserve of 800 to Nairobi, Kenya, and the United States deployed 300 special operations troops to Bujumbura, Burundi, as a contingency force and to assist foreign nationals evacuating Rwanda southward by road.[55] What is unclear is whether such lightly equipped troops could have quickly quashed violence in the capital and, if so, whether genocide would have stopped elsewhere.

The mere presence of Western troops was insufficient to quell violence, as indicated by the fact that killing continued in the capital during the evacuation. The Western evacuators thus would have had to confront the interim government's forces, which in Kigali alone consisted of about 2,000 elite and 4,000 regular army troops equipped with heavy weapons, 1,000 national police, and 2,000 militia.[56] Facing these 9,000 or so Rwandan government forces would have been 1,400 Western troops who lacked logistics, were unfamiliar with the terrain, possessed few armored vehicles or heavy weapons, and had to commit more than half their forces merely to guard the airport on the outskirts of town and several key meeting points.

The extremely limited number of these interveners who were available for combat and their lack of preparation for such hostilities is illustrated by the French contingent. The French evacuation force comprising about 450 troops was built around three paratroop infantry companies. One secured the airport, a second secured the French embassy and several meeting points, and the third provided escort and rapid reaction capability. The actual extraction of foreign nationals was carried out by a few additional specialized detachments totaling perhaps 100 troops. Available intelligence was "mediocre," according to an official French account. The French troops possessed antitank weapons, but not armored vehicles because "the speed of the operation did not permit transport" of such heavy materiel in the airlift. For ground transport, French troops relied mainly on "vehicles abandoned by UNAMIR." The rapid pace of the French deployment to Rwanda, with lead forces arriving less than three days after Habyarimana's death, was expedited not merely by the French troops already being positioned at nearby bases in Africa, but by the airlift's absence of heavy weapons, vehicles, and logistics necessary for combat operations or a prolonged stay. Similarly, the Belgian paratroopers who arrived the day after the initial French contingent devoted themselves mainly to guarding the airport, leaving the job of finding and escorting expatriates to the Belgian battalion of UNAMIR. Thus, of the 1,400 Western troops in Kigali during the first week of genocide, only a few hundred dared venture away from the airport or some other fixed site.[57]

If these lightly equipped evacuators had attempted to conduct offensive operations and the Rwandan government's 9,000 armed fighters in Kigali had resisted, the Western troops likely would have suffered significant casualties until being reinforced or withdrawn. Also posing a threat was the RPF, which explicitly threatened to attack Belgian and French evacuators if they extended the scope or duration of their mission. The rebel group declared on April 9, 1994, that it would engage French troops if they did more than evacuate foreign nationals, and threatened to attack Belgian evacuators if they did not depart by April 14. The RPF already had in the capital approximately 1,000 troops when violence renewed—600 stationed there legally under the Arusha agreement and about another 400 who had been infiltrated—as well as about 1,000 clandestine civilian supporters. In addition, RPF reinforcements from the north began arriving in Kigali rapidly on April 12, 1994.[58] The Tutsi rebels also possessed surface-to-air missiles capable of shooting down Western resupply aircraft, as authorities in Brussels knew and feared. Belgium's foreign minister, Willy Claes, later testified: "The RPF told us very clearly that it agreed to a short humanitarian evacuation operation, but it was necessary not to transform peacekeeping into peacemaking; otherwise, it would consider us enemies. . . . Nothing is easier than shooting down an airplane. This played a primary role in our decision-making at the governmental level and in our consultations with the UN."[59]

It is conceivable that a demonstration of Western resolve would have compelled extremist Hutu leaders or their followers, or both, to halt organized violence in the capital. French troops might have cajoled their erstwhile FAR allies to desist. Belgian troops, whom the Hutu extremists viewed as enemies, potentially could have intimidated the FAR with a show of force and threats that they would escalate as soon as reinforcements arrived. The strongest evidence for this best-case scenario is that on the one occasion when UNAMIR soldiers did fire on a group of menacing Rwandan soldiers and militia outside a stadium in Kigali, on April 7, they killed fifteen and managed to disperse the rest of the group. However, this single UN attack bought only a one-day respite from violence near the stadium, and it did not stop the harassment of peacekeepers from continuing in the rest of the city. Accordingly, this example actually demonstrates that the extremists could not be deterred by a small show of force. Moreover, as noted, neither UNAMIR nor the Western evacuation forces were equipped to prevail in a prolonged military confrontation.[60]

Finally, the most important consideration in evaluating this claim is that France and Belgium perceived each other as sympathizing with opposite sides in the civil war—which would have made a joint operation extremely unlikely. France supported the Hutu-led government while Belgium was perceived to sympathize with the Tutsi-led RPF, a difference that led to serious tensions between French and Belgian nationals in Rwanda before the genocide. On January 11, 1994, Belgium's military intelligence agency reported that French advisers, who stayed behind after the withdrawal of French troops from Rwanda, were "organizing a campaign of denigrating the Belgian peacekeepers." Following Habyarimana's assassination, the French embassy reportedly spread the rumor that Belgian troops had shot down the president's plane. After Rwandan soldiers killed ten Belgian peacekeepers on April 7, France continued to supply arms to the Rwandan army. Indeed, the aircraft that brought French evacuation troops to Kigali two days later also carried weapons for delivery to the Rwandan army. France even went so far as to consider using its evacuation troops to bolster the FAR—a far cry from reining it in.[61]

Thus the Reyntjens proposal would have required an immediate and complete reversal of French policy, switching from arming the FAR to confronting it with force. Considering that foreign policy rarely reverses so quickly, it is highly unlikely that Belgian and French troops could have worked together to conduct an enforcement mission. One alternative would have been for Belgium to conduct the mission alone by airlifting its 800-man reserve from Nairobi to bolster the 860 troops it had in Kigali during the evacuation. A 1,660-troop Belgian force could have been at least as effective as a multinational force of 1,400. The other alternative would have been an exclusively French intervention, which might have been more successful at eliciting moderation from the extremists. Strangely, such unilateral interventions, which are far more plausible in light of the differing viewpoints in Paris and Brussels, are rarely if ever cited as missed opportunities.

Finally, even if France and Belgium had somehow managed to overcome their differences to implement the Reyntjens proposal, with some or all of the evacuators expanding their mission and succeeding in restoring order in Kigali, they still might not have averted genocide in the countryside. By April 10, Tutsi across much of Rwanda had already assembled at central sites, and large massacres were beginning. The evacuation forces had neither means to deploy sufficient troops quickly to the countryside nor equipment and logistics to conduct operations there. The subsequent experience of Operation Turquoise suggests that once large-scale rural killing began it would have continued until foreign troops arrived on the scene to stop it[62]—unless extremist leaders in Kigali had ordered a nationwide halt. These ringleaders might have issued such orders spontaneously upon a forceful Western intervention in Kigali, but they also could have chosen to let the rural genocide run its course, directing the army and national police to continue attacking Tutsi assemblages.

Some observers, including Alison Des Forges, believe that stopping the genocide in the capital would have been sufficient to avert it entirely: "Because the operation of the genocide was highly centralized, stopping the killing in Kigali would have quickly quelled violence elsewhere in the country. . . . Any serious challenge from foreign troops would have signaled that the interim government was illegitimate in the eyes of the international community and unlikely to receive the support it would need to survive . . . This would have discouraged Rwandans from joining the killing campaign."[63] However, there is strong evidence to the contrary. Most telling, not even the subsequent international condemnation represented by the combination of an arms embargo, economic sanctions, and Operation Turquoise proved sufficient to halt the killing campaign. Moreover, the genocide did not have completely unitary command. For example, extremist radio RTLM urged its audience to kill Tutsi as soon as they were captured, while the interim government called for Tutsi to be held until arrival of the army. In addition, several Kigali officials fought each other to direct strategy, and important elements of implementation were left to local officials. All of this suggests that there was not a single leader who could have pulled the plug on the entire campaign.[64]

The only way for interveners in Kigali to have had a firm chance of stopping the genocide nationwide would have been to capture the main ringleaders and coerce them to issue public orders to their supporters to halt the killing. However, before the interveners could even have attempted such coercion, they would have had to know that genocide was occurring outside the capital, which was not apparent to most Westerners in Kigali at the time. Moreover, although Belgian officials knew generally who was directing the violence in the capital,[65] capturing Bagosora and his allies would not have been a simple matter. In an analogous hunt in 1993, U.S. troops failed to find Somali warlord Mohammed Farah Aideed and suffered significant casualties in their efforts. In Panama in 1990, U.S. troops needed four days to locate President Manuel Noriega and two weeks to negotiate his surrender.[66] In Rwanda, Western forces were so lightly equipped that extremist Hutu leaders could have eluded capture for a long time, while genocide continued at a torrid pace in the countryside, where 95 percent of Rwandans lived.

More Robust Peacekeeping

I have argued in previous writings that if UNAMIR had been reinforced several months before the outbreak of violence, as Belgium's government urged at the time, genocide might have been averted.[67] Such a reinforcement was justified by the flood of warning signs from Rwanda—available primarily to Belgium and France but often shared with the UN and United States— which indicated that extremist elements were seeking to provoke renewed civil war and massive civilian killing, if not necessarily genocide. (For details, see next chapter.) As early as January 1994, Belgium's Foreign Ministry sought to enlarge or replace the UN mandate on the grounds that it was overly restrictive, especially the requirement that peacekeepers consult Rwanda's national police before conducting security operations. As Belgium's ambassador to Rwanda explained in a cable to Brussels on January 13: "If the police themselves are implicated in the activities of the Interahamwe, this type of consultation has little chance of success." When Belgium's initial efforts at the UN failed, Foreign Minister Claes wrote Boutros-Ghali on February 11, warning that unless security were enhanced Rwanda could suffer an "irreversible explosion of violence." On February 24, Brussels directed its UN delegate to try again to win support for a stronger force on the grounds that "UNAMIR cannot, under its current mandate, establish 'solid maintenance of public order.'" The delegate replied that the United States and United Kingdom opposed any change in UNAMIR's mandate, force level, or rules of engagement because of concerns about the expense and danger of transforming the mission from consensual peacekeeping to confrontational peace enforcement. In response to all these efforts, Belgium received only a trivial concession: 200 Ghanaian peacekeepers were redeployed to Kigali from the northern demilitarized zone. Trying once again in mid-March 1994, Belgium's defense minister, Léo Delcroix, proposed during a visit to Rwanda that the UN Security Council should bolster the rules of engagement for UNAMIR at its next reauthorization on April 5. However, the rules were not changed at that meeting, and the genocide started the following day.[68]

Given that reinforcing an existing peacekeeping operation to prevent the renewal of civil war is less likely to result in casualties than deploying troops into combat to stop a war once it has restarted, this preventive option should generally be more acceptable to casualty-averse Western publics. In Rwanda, additional peacekeepers with the proper equipment, mandate, and rules of engagement could have deterred the outbreak of killing or at least snuffed it out early. Appropriate reinforcement would have required about 3,500 additional high-quality troops in Kigali, armored personnel carriers, helicopters, adequate logistics, and prior authorization to use force to seize weapons and ensure security without consulting Rwandan police. Essentially, this would have been the 5,000-troop force that Dallaire envisioned but deployed *before* the genocide, so that it could take preventive action before the violence got out of hand.[69]

Under Chapter VI of the UN Charter, which governs consensual peacekeeping operations such as UNAMIR, Rwanda's government would have had to consent to such a change. The only alternative would have been to obtain a Chapter VII authorization from the UN Security Council to permit military intervention without consent; but in the absence of an acute security or humanitarian emergency, Russia or China probably would have vetoed such a proposal as excessive intrusion into the internal affairs of a sovereign state. However, it probably would not have been necessary to resort to Chapter VII because Rwanda's government likely would have consented to the expansion of UNAMIR before the genocide. At the time, prior to Habyarimana's plane crash and the extremist takeover, Rwanda's cabinet was still dominated by opposition moderates who had negotiated the Arusha accords, which called for a neutral international force to "guarantee overall security of the country." Indeed, it was the UN Security Council, not Rwanda, that had watered down the implementation of this provision in the mission's mandate, ultimately authorizing UNAMIR only to "contribute to the security of the city of Kigali."[70] As tensions mounted in early 1994, the moderate-dominated Rwandan government again asked the United Nations to dismantle armed irregulars—meaning the militias that, unlike the Rwandan army and RPF, were not recognized under the Arusha accords. However, because the peacekeepers had no hope of accomplishing such a task with their weak contingent, the United Nations was forced to decline the request on the grounds that the mission was too dangerous.[71] Thus it appears that the Rwandan government would have welcomed a reinforcement of UNAMIR before violence broke out—in effect allowing the United Nations to take over control of the capital to protect it from both Hutu extremists and Tutsi rebels. Of course, extremist Hutu elements might not have viewed so benignly the UN reinforcements, especially if they were Belgian troops, and might have responded by attacking the peacekeepers or even attempting to start the genocide. Still, so long as Habyarimana and the moderate opposition remained alive and in control of the government, there was a good chance that UNAMIR could have been reinforced consensually. This opportunity evaporated when Habyarimana and the moderates were assassinated during the first two days of killing.

The remaining question is whether such a beefed-up intervention force deployed before the renewal of violence could have prevented the genocide. Most likely, if reinforced peacekeepers had attempted offensive operations before the genocide, they would have confronted resistance. In fact, Bagosora tested UNAMIR's will in just this manner in February 1994. As Belgian troops approached an armed gang at his house, he ordered his men to aim their weapons at the Belgians, who backed down.[72] By contrast, had a reinforced UNAMIR faced down extremists in such initial incidents, demonstrating the will and capability for combat, the genocide plot might have been shelved. Even if the extremists had still attempted to launch the genocide, the peacekeepers might have been strong enough to quash it in Kigali during the first few days. Five thousand troops in the capital would have represented more than sixteen per thousand of population, a level that historically has been sufficient to quell severe civil disorders around the world—although the force's capacity to keep order would have depended on the extent to which the Rwandan army, police, militias, or rebels had decided to engage it in combat. If the peacekeepers had been able to protect moderate Hutu leaders and Tutsi in the capital and capture some of the extremists during the first days of violence, they might have significantly reduced the chance of mass killing taking off in the countryside. Though Tutsi in the countryside were being terrorized and chased to central gathering sites starting April 7, the large-scale massacres there did not begin until about April 11. Quashing genocide in Kigali before then might have prevented the rural massacres from ever starting in earnest.

Thus the early reinforcement of UNAMIR is the only proposed action that would have had a good chance of averting the killing. This option would not have been foolproof because extremists in Kigali and elsewhere might have reacted to the announcement of forthcoming UN reinforcements by attempting to launch the genocide preventively in early 1994, before the extra peacekeepers could arrive. Even if they had done so, however, the outcome would have been better for Rwanda's Tutsi than if intervention had been launched after the outbreak of genocide, because the additional peacekeepers would have benefited from a head start in deploying to stop the violence.[73]

CHAPTER NINE

Early Warning and
Preventive Intervention

A KEY DETERMINANT of the ultimate effectiveness of any military intervention in Rwanda would have been how early it was launched. Only by reinforcing the peacekeepers early in 1994, well before the outbreak of genocide, could intervention have stood a good chance of averting genocide. Barring that, the sooner intervention was launched after the killing started, the more lives would have been saved.

As noted in chapter 1, there is a growing consensus among American policymakers that humanitarian military intervention should be launched to stop genocide when such violence comes to light, especially where intervention can save lives at low cost. In the case of Rwanda, however, even a policy of reacting immediately to evidence of genocide would have been insufficient to save most of the victims. To be more successful, a lower threshold for action would have been required, perhaps authorizing intervention as soon as the risk of genocide was deemed sufficiently high. To assess this possibility, it is useful to explore whether the international community had sufficient advance warning in Rwanda to know that a genocide was likely before the outbreak of violence on April 6, 1994, or at least to recognize immediately that this initial outburst was the start of genocide.

Such questions are complicated by the fact that different international actors had varying access to intelligence before the genocide. France was tapping phones in Kigali, including those of foreign embassies, and so presumably had at least as much information as any other foreign entity. According to one expert, however, France's surveillance efforts focused mainly on the RPF rather than on Hutu extremists and so may have overlooked indicators of genocide.[1] Belgium's defense intelligence agency had three or four staff members following central Africa, who processed raw intelligence about Rwanda from a variety of sources: Belgium's embassy in Kigali; its military technical-cooperation mission there; radio stations that were monitored by the embassy; and the White Fathers religious order, which faxed in daily reports.[2]

In addition, UNAMIR had two intelligence cells, both manned by Belgians but not authorized by the United Nations. (The UN had rejected Belgium's request to establish a formal intelligence structure on the grounds it was inappropriately "offensive" for a peacekeeping mission.) The "battalion-level" cell reported only to Belgium and did not share top-secret intelligence with Dallaire or his "force-level" cell, which reported to him and prepared daily situation reports for UN headquarters in New York. Further inhibiting the Belgians from sharing intelligence with the UN was the fact that the force-level intelligence briefings in Rwanda were chaired by a Bengali who spoke English rather than French or Dutch.[3]

The United States had only one defense attaché in the region who was based in Cameroon and had responsibility for at least two other countries besides Rwanda. However, the U.S. ambassador in Kigali appears to have been briefed regularly by Dallaire, as well as by the Belgian and French embassies. Outside Kigali, no substantial sharing of intelligence on Rwanda appears to have occurred between Belgium, France, and the United States, at least up to the outbreak of violence. Thus France probably had the best intelligence, followed in descending order by Belgium, the United States, Dallaire, and UN headquarters in New York, which was relatively in the dark.[4] Dallaire later confirmed: "A lot of the world powers were all there with their embassies and their military attaches. And you can't tell me those bastards didn't have a lot of information. They would never pass that information on to me, ever."[5]

By far the most is known about intelligence available to Belgium, because a subsequent Belgian Senate investigation examined all classified documents from the four months immediately preceding the genocide. These documents reveal that Belgium's defense intelligence agency, by February 1994, had obtained solid information about extremist plots. Indeed, all of the Belgian intelligence reports discussed below, except in one case as noted, were rated highly reliable.[6] However, the agency had no trained intelligence personnel in Rwanda, and UNAMIR's battalion-level cell was not a formal intelligence unit. Thus Brussels was unable to obtain some basic elements of political intelligence, such as whether it was the Rwandan government or the rebels who were responsible for delaying implementation of the Arusha accords.[7]

Numerous reports of ethnic violence in Rwanda surfaced in the months and years preceding the genocide. Death squads were exposed in 1992, and death lists containing hundreds of names came to light in the succeeding two years.[8] In spring 1992 the Belgian embassy in Kigali reported an anonymous allegation of a "secret headquarters charged with exterminating the Tutsi of Rwanda to resolve definitively, in their manner, the ethnic problem in Rwanda and to crush the domestic Hutu opposition." In March 1993 an international human rights panel reported that most victims of sporadic massacres in Rwanda were killed because they were Tutsi. During the first week of December 1993 several ominous indications arose: a Belgian cable reported the Presidential Guard conducting paramilitary training of youths; a Rwandan journal reported weapons being distributed to militias; and UNAMIR received an anonymous but credible letter, purportedly from leading moderate Rwandan army officers, warning of a "Machiavellian plan" to conduct massacres throughout the country, starting in areas of high Tutsi concentration and also targeting leading opposition politicians. On December 17 the Rwandan press exposed details of a planned "final solution," including militia coordination, transportation arrangements, French military aid, and "identification committees" to compile death lists. These dangers signs were usually conveyed to Brussels within days via cable—the anonymous letter on December 14 and the press report of a final solution on December 23, 1993.[9]

Soon after, UNAMIR was contacted by an informant known as Jean-Pierre, whose accusations spurred Dallaire to send his famous cable to UN headquarters in New York on January 11, 1994, warning of reported paramilitary training, weapons caches, and extermination squads. On January 13, General Dallaire also shared this information at a meeting with the American, Belgian, and French ambassadors, as well as the UN secretary general's special representative, Jacques-Roger Booh-Booh. Remarkably, all three embassies denied the informant the asylum he requested. (Thus the repeated allegation that the United Nations had secret intelligence in the "genocide fax," which it failed to act on or share with member states, is a gross exaggeration.)[10] In mid-January a "desk-level analysis" by the U.S. Central Intelligence Agency predicted that, in the worst of three scenarios if civil war resumed, more than a half-million Rwandans could die.[11]

Also in mid-January 1994, Belgium's embassy reported that both the rebels and Rwanda's prime minister, a moderate member of the Hutu opposition, feared that President Habyarimana might be complicit in the Machiavellian plan for general destabilization. On February 2, Belgium's defense intelligence agency reported that the Interahamwe, supported by the government, had been tasked to locate all Tutsi families. In a particularly prescient cable on February 25, Belgium's foreign affairs minister, Willy Claes, warned that the deteriorating situation "could well lead to a new bloodbath . . . it would be unacceptable for public opinion if Belgian peacekeepers in Rwanda were to be passive witnesses to a genocide." On March 1 the Belgian embassy reported that RTLM was broadcasting "inflammatory declarations calling for hatred—even extermination—of the other [Tutsi] ethnic component of the population."[12]

On March 2 the moderate Hutu prime minister told Belgian troops that militias were established throughout Rwanda's hundreds of cellules, except in the prefecture of Gitarama. Around March 20 a top FAR officer told an official in Belgium's military assistance program that he was ready to "liquidate" Tutsi if the Arusha accords were implemented. Finally, on April 4, 1994, two days before Habyarimana's assassination, Colonel Bagosora told a meeting that included Dallaire, Booh-Booh, and Belgium's top peace-keeper, Colonel Luc Marchal: "The only plausible solution for Rwanda would be elimination of the Tutsi." Marchal later testified that in light of "the number and the precision of details" that had come to light by this time, he "had no doubt" what was being prepared and expected "tens of thousands of deaths."[13]

However, scholars of "warning-response" long have noted that though hindsight is 20/20, such early warning signals often are recognized only in retrospect. Indeed, before Rwanda's genocide there were strong reasons to dismiss the risk of such violence. First, much of the intelligence was incomplete and thus appeared inconsistent with a plan for nationwide genocide. For example, the genocide fax reported the Interahamwe numbering 1,700, which was far too few for a nationwide killing campaign. A Belgian diplomatic cable before the genocide, based on the same informant, reported an even lower estimate of only 600–900 Interahamwe. During the genocide, the actual number of militia was sixty times larger than the low end of this Belgian estimate and some twenty times larger than even the higher estimate in the genocide fax. Because of such faulty intelligence, the greatest fear expressed by Belgium's battalion-level intelligence officer as late as March 2, 1994, was a campaign to exterminate Tutsi in Kigali. Although this was a serious threat, the capital contained only 4 percent of Rwanda's population.

Many early warnings were dismissed as not credible. For example, the information in the genocide fax initially was rated by Belgian intelligence officials as F6—the lowest reliability.[14] In addition, as Prunier notes, because death lists often consisted of handwritten names in notebooks, UNAMIR officials tended to discount them. In some cases, these lists were merely the membership rolls of opposition political parties, which ironically had been prepared by the moderate leaders themselves to justify their claim to seats in the forthcoming legislature that was to be based on proportional representation.[15]

Adding to the confusion, many of the warning signs appeared to signal an impending renewal of civil war rather than a killing campaign. Numerous Belgian cables reported that Colonel Bagosora and the militias intended to provoke such renewed war in order to prevent the implementation of the Arusha accords. The anonymous letter from moderate FAR officers on December 3, 1993, warned of a plan "to incite the RPF to violate the cease-fire, as it did in February 1993, which will then give a pretext for the general resumption of hostilities." Belgium's defense intelligence agency issued the same warning on December 28, 1993, citing a meeting that Bagosora attended on December 10. The warning of renewed civil war was repeated in a Belgian briefing in late January 1994. On February 9 a Belgian cable reported the same concern being expressed by RPF President Alexis Kanyarengwe: "The goal cannot be but to provoke bloody troubles at an opportune moment to prevent implementation of the Arusha accords."[16] UNAMIR's deputy commander, in his memoirs, portrays a scene in early 1994 that resembles a prototypical security dilemma spiraling inexorably toward renewed war, as each side took precautionary measures against imminent attack that made the other side fear such an attack.[17] Even hate radio appeared to signal an impending two-sided civil war, with RTLM's calls for civil violence being countered by rebel radio's appeals for an armed popular uprising. Although the potential renewal of civil war troubled the West, it was not the same as impending genocide.

Even many close observers of Rwanda doubted warnings of looming genocide, in part because of previous false alarms. As Gérard Prunier later testified: "In the region, everyone has been regularly circulating plans of genocide and assassination for the past thirty years. From time to time, one of them materialized. . . . But for twenty-two years this had not happened, and one came to believe that things had calmed down." Moreover, immediately before the genocide, most warnings of impending massacres in December, January, and March had not panned out, calling into question the existence of any "final solution" plot.[18] The U.S. State Department's political-military adviser for the region at the time, Colonel Tony Marley, likewise says he "tended to discredit" the information in the genocide fax "because we had heard allegations of genocide, or warnings of genocide, pertaining to Rwanda dating back at least to 1992"—the year he assumed responsibility for the region. "We had heard them cry wolf so many times" that the new warnings fell on deaf ears.[19] Belgian peacekeepers responsible for intelligence dismissed the warnings to such an extent that they requested their wives join them in Rwanda.[20] General Dallaire himself, barely a week before Habyarimana's assassination, assured Belgium's UN delegation that he doubted the existence of any "master plan" aimed at confrontation in Rwanda.[21]

Most close observers also relied on two assumptions that seemed to rule out the prospect of genocide. First, President Habyarimana was seen as a relative moderate who would contain the extreme elements of his inner circle. In five Belgian cables from January 31 to March 18, 1994, Habyarimana was portrayed as making good-faith efforts to implement the Arusha accords, in contrast to other politicians.[22] Colonel Vincent, in charge of Belgium's military cooperation with the FAR from 1991 to 1994 and perhaps the Belgian most intimately familiar with Rwandan security affairs, recalls: "Habyarimana was respected and had control of the system, which enabled him to limit the earlier massacres. . . . Nobody foresaw the assassination of the president, and that is what tipped Rwanda into the horror." A second assumption was that even extremists would act in their own rational self-interest, so if the civil war resumed, they would concentrate on fending off the rebels' military offensive. Instead, as events transpired, these Hutu devoted most of their resources to exterminating Tutsi civilians, at the price of largely ignoring the war effort and thereby facilitating the RPA's lightning victory over them. As Gérard Prunier notes, this was an irrational strategy eerily reminiscent of Hitler, whose "genocide of the Jews undermined the German war effort in World War II."[23]

Even after the fact, the "inevitability" of the Rwandan genocide is not clear, because mystery still surrounds the shooting down of Habyarimana's plane, which set off the killing. If the plane was shot down by Hutu extremists, then there was probably a premeditated plan to trigger and perpetrate the genocide, which made its outbreak inevitable in the absence of prior intervention. However, if the missile was launched by Tutsi rebels to kill the recalcitrant president and as a first step in renewing their offensive, then the genocide plot may have been merely a Hutu contingency plan, inadvertently triggered by the Tutsi attack. Accusations of RPF responsibility for the assassination were renewed in early 2000 by the leak of an August 1997 UN memorandum, in which three Tutsi were reported to have confessed to participating in the attack as part of an RPF strike team. On the basis of this information and further testimony from RPF defectors, a French judge investigating the case was reported in October 2000 to be planning to issue an international arrest warrant for Paul Kagame, rebel commander at the time of the attack and president of Rwanda since April 2000. [24] If Tutsi rebels did shoot down the plane, then the eventual genocide may not have been inevitable after all, which would offer a further explanation of the West's failure to anticipate it.

Whatever the reason, the fact is that the foreigners most closely involved in Rwanda prior to the genocide did not see it coming. For example, Colonel Vincent testified that before Habyarimana's assassination he had "never received serious indications of genocide." Belgium's defense intelligence chief, Major General Verschoore, testified that his agency "perceived some signs of serious problems but certainly wasn't able to conclude from the information received that a genocide was being prepared." His director for central Africa, Major Hock, testified: "We didn't foresee a genocide but only some bumps in the implementation of Arusha that could lead to thousands of victims. . . . Nobody could imagine that which would happen. An intelligence service is not a fortune teller." Even a staunch critic of the West's failure to intervene in Rwanda, Astri Suhrke, concludes that "nobody could imagine the speed and size of the genocide that developed."[25]

Close foreign observers did, however, understand the risk that extremists might provoke renewal of civil war that could lead to thousands of civilian casualties. It was this danger that motivated Belgium to seek a reinforcement of UNAMIR in the UN Security Council in early 1994. Such reinforcement before the renewal of civil war, with the welcome of the host government, would have been a relatively low-risk endeavor with the potential to avert severe anticipated violence. Remarkably, the U.S. and U.K. governments have never acknowledged or offered justification for blocking Belgium's efforts to gain UN authorization for this preventive reinforcement. In addition, as of this writing in early 2001, the United States retains the same peacekeeping policy that compelled it to block Belgium's efforts in 1994.

Although foreign observers did not foresee the genocide, after the outbreak of violence on April 6, 1994, a few of them appear almost immediately to have recognized the beginning of a massive anti-Tutsi campaign, if not its eventual extent. For example, on April 8, 1994, senior French military officers reportedly projected that 100,000 Tutsi would die in the violence at a point when only a few thousand had been killed so far. This prediction reflected some understanding of the dynamics of the violence even if it underestimated the ultimate toll by a factor of five.[26]

However, this reported French prediction was not conveyed to the U.S. government at the time, and there is no evidence that other close observers shared this appreciation of what was happening, despite the retrospective assertions of some human rights advocates.[27] For example, Human Rights Watch now claims that during the first days of violence, when mainly Hutu were being killed, informed observers of Rwanda must have known that an anti-Tutsi genocide was occurring: "Surely they must have understood what was happening by late on April 7." The reality is that not even Human Rights Watch itself appreciated the genocide during the first few days. Indeed, in an op-ed article published in the *Washington Post* on April 17, 1994—eleven days into the violence—the group failed to warn even of the risk of genocide.[28]

Human Rights Watch now says that the risk of genocide was obvious because of the intermittent but persistent massacres that had been carried out with impunity against Tutsi since the RPF invasion of October 1990. However, the organization's own statistics indicate that during the three and a half years of civil war before the genocide only about 2,000 Tutsi civilians had been killed—a rate of about fifty per month. Such a level of killing rightly caused concern, but it did not suggest that the death rate would suddenly jump to 250,000 in the following month.

Human Rights Watch also cites the January 1994 CIA analysis, which estimated that up to a half-million Tutsi could die if violence resumed in Rwanda, as evidence that the White House knew immediately after Habyarimana's assassination that a genocide would occur. However, the CIA study contained three possible scenarios, only one of which predicted such mass killings. Intelligence analysts routinely include such a worst-case scenario to cover themselves in case events go awry. Moreover, such "desk-level" analyses seldom if ever reach the president. U.S. officials did know, within two days after the Rwandan president's plane was shot down, about the bloody coup, the large-scale violence in the capital, and the renewed civil war. But they also expected the Tutsi rebels to win quickly. There is no reason to believe that President Clinton or any of his senior advisers knew immediately of the nationwide genocide.

Most other foreign observers with access to classified intelligence also did not recognize the genocidal nature of the violence immediately upon its outbreak. For example, Foreign Minister Claes of Belgium testified that conflicting reports of violence during the first two weeks prevented any definitive judgment: "To conclude that a genocide was under way . . . that is a leap I could not make" as of April 17, when the last Belgian troops were withdrawn. As Des Forges notes, U.S. and UN officials similarly were "misinterpreting the real nature of the slaughter . . . [by relying on] familiar formulae borrowed from other situations where violence against civilians had accompanied war. . . . [T]he problem was not just the speed of events but their extraordinary nature." This type of misperception bedeviled many close observers of Rwanda.[29]

In some respects, it is easier to understand the West's failure to intervene immediately upon the outbreak of violence—when the situation looked like renewed civil war—than its earlier reluctance to reinforce UNAMIR while Rwanda was still at peace. Whereas a small preventive reinforcement might have deterred the outbreak of fighting, many more troops and probably casualties would have been required to stop the war after it started, which potentially could have put in doubt Western public support. In addition, although both sides in Rwanda probably would have welcomed an earlier preventive reinforcement, after the outbreak of violence the extremist Hutu immediately killed ten Belgian troops and the rebels issued threats to attack Western troops if they intervened in the civil war. Even if interveners had faced down this threat successfully and managed to stop the fighting, it is not apparent how or when peacekeepers could have departed Rwanda without the war's resuming. Furthermore, deploying ground troops to an ongoing civil war would have set an unsustainable precedent; there are simply too many such conflicts around the world to permit prolonged intervention in every case. Although Rwanda was a special case because of the genocidal nature of its violence, this did not become apparent until later. Even the limited option of air power, which in retrospect could have saved many lives, was not an obvious choice in the confusing circumstances of early April 1994. During civil war, bombing can inadvertently exacerbate fighting and civilian atrocities, as NATO's 1999 air campaign did in Kosovo.

None of this analysis is intended to justify the West's inaction in Rwanda after the outbreak of violence, especially given that the UN had committed itself to ensuring Rwandan security and that many local actors were relying on this commitment. However, this discussion does show that immediate intervention to stop the violence was neither an obvious nor a risk-free option, especially in light of the information available at the time. By contrast, prior to the genocide the cost-benefit analysis should have weighed heavily in favor of reinforcing the peacekeepers preventively. Rwanda was known to be at high risk for renewal of violence, yet was also a fairly small country in which a robust contingent of peacekeepers with liberal rules of engagement would have had a good chance of maintaining order. In this regard, it was an ideal candidate for a preventive reinforcement—that never occurred.

CHAPTER TEN

Lessons

A REALISTIC U.S. military intervention launched as soon as President Clinton could have determined that genocide was being attempted in Rwanda would not have averted the genocide. It could, however, have saved an estimated 75,000 to 125,000 Tutsi from death, about 15 to 25 percent of those who ultimately lost their lives, in addition to tens of thousands of Hutu. Rwanda represents a particularly tough case for intervention in some respects, including its rapid rate of killing and inaccessible location. However, it would have been relatively easy in other respects, such as the limited military strength of potential adversaries and the country's small size. By contrast, humanitarian intervention is much more challenging in a country with the population and territory of Congo, or the armed forces of the former Yugoslavia.

Though each case is different, Rwanda offers several lessons about humanitarian military intervention more generally. First and most obvious, such intervention is no substitute for prevention. Even an ideal intervention in Rwanda after the killing started would have left hundreds of thousands of Tutsi dead. This observation is not intended to justify the West's failure to intervene in Rwanda after the genocide came to light. However, it does underscore that to avert such disasters completely there is no alternative to the time-consuming business of diplomacy and negotiation. Unfortunately, as I have explained in previous writings, such efforts by the international community in Rwanda before the genocide were ill-conceived and counterproductive.[1] Western powers pressured the Hutu government of Rwanda to sign a peace agreement that in effect handed over power to the opposing Tutsi rebels. This surrender threatened the vital interests of the entrenched extremist Hutu elite, who perceived the mass killing of Tutsi as the only way to retain power and avoid retribution. Had the international community intended to promote genocide, it could hardly have devised a better strategy. The clear lesson is that the best way to stop genocide is not military intervention after the fact but wise diplomacy that prevents genocide from starting in the first place.

Second, when the international community pressures civil war combatants to sign a peace agreement that leaves one or both sides vulnerable, the only way to insure against a renewal of violence is to deploy a robust peace enforcement mission preventively. In Rwanda such a mission might have been deployed successfully immediately after the signing of the Arusha accords in August 1993, or even perhaps as late as February 1994, when Belgium urged the UN Security Council to beef up the manpower and mandate of the existing small, lightly armed peacekeeping mission. However, in the wake of the Somalia debacle of October 1993, the United States and United Kingdom blocked all attempts to deploy an enforcement mission to Rwanda. If a robust mission had been deployed preventively, it might have reduced the fear among the Hutu elite of impending retribution at the hands of the Tutsi and thereby reduced their motivation to launch the genocide. One scholar who has analyzed a number of similar cases characterizes this type of fear as the "critical barrier to civil war settlement" and argues that it can be overcome only by credible third-party commitments to enforcing peace.[2] If a peace enforcement mission had been deployed preventively to Rwanda but extremist Hutu had launched the genocide anyway, the peacekeepers at least could have commenced efforts immediately to halt the fighting, without the protracted delays associated with airlifting additional troops and equipment to the theater. This crucial time savings would have increased significantly the chances of stanching the violence in its early stages.

Third, statesmen, whether pursuing prevention or intervention, must use their imagination to better anticipate the behavior of foreign actors. In Rwanda, Western officials did not foresee the genocide despite numerous warning signs, in part because the act was so immoral that it was difficult for them to imagine. The harsh reality is that if ruthless political actors perceive self-interest in mass murder or forced migration, they are willing to perpetrate it. This is most likely when entrenched authoritarian leaders in ethnically divided societies face the prospect of losing power and suffering potentially deadly retribution for past offenses, which can make genocide and ethnic cleansing appear the only way of retaining power and protecting themselves. In recognition of this risk, when a peacekeeping force is deployed preventively to a fragile area like Rwanda that is undergoing a political transition, it should be adequately sized and equipped to stop incipient violence, not merely a lightly armed tripwire that serves mainly to foster a false sense of security.

Fourth, if the West is unwilling to deploy robust forces preventively, it must temper its use of coercive diplomacy against ethnically stratified states intended to compel rulers to surrender power overnight, so as not to inadvertently trigger massive violence. In just the past few years, ill-conceived Western diplomacy based mainly on the threat of economic sanctions or bombing has provoked a tragic backlash not just in Rwanda but also in Kosovo and East Timor, as local rulers opted to inflict massive violence rather than hand over power or territory to lifelong enemies. In each case, Western military intervention arrived too late to prevent widespread atrocities.[3] As long as the West lacks the will for large-scale preventive deployments, its diplomats should avoid such risky coercion and instead concentrate on providing incentives, including economic assistance, to such states in return for their moving gradually toward interethnic power-sharing. The West also should be prepared to offer "golden parachutes"—monetary rewards, asylum, and immunity from subsequent prosecution—to entrenched authorities who consent to leave power peacefully. While human rights groups abjure the prospect of cutting deals with leaders who have blood on their hands, in some cases forgiving past crimes may be the price of preventing future ones.

Fifth, once humanitarian military intervention is deemed necessary, time becomes of the essence because most violence can be perpetrated in a matter of weeks, as also demonstrated by the cases of Rwanda, Kosovo, and East Timor. Realistically, however, domestic political considerations make it unlikely that the West will ever launch a maximum intervention so quickly. Thus U.S. defense planners, who have greater resources at their disposal than the rest of the world combined, should exercise creativity to develop alternative deployment strategies to address such situations. The case of Rwanda underscores that lighter intervention options, which avoid combat areas and focus mainly on stopping violence against civilians, could save many lives if pursued seriously and expeditiously. Pentagon resources should be committed to developing such options, especially if ground-troop deployments are ruled out for fear of potential casualties. To expedite intervention, the Pentagon also should prepare advance contingency plans for known trouble spots.

In addition, before and during any crisis, national security officials should better coordinate intelligence held by domestic and foreign allied intelligence agencies—and open sources such as foreign media and nongovernmental organizations that may have contacts throughout the troubled region and nearby refugee camps—to determine in a timely manner the nature of prospective violence and possible remedies.[4] In the case of Rwanda, it appears that one U.S. intelligence agency did obtain a fairly accurate picture of the violence almost immediately upon its outbreak but was unable to convey this understanding to the rest of the American government. The main problem appears to have been information overload—that is, too much rather than too little intelligence. According to a State Department official, this is a perennial problem: "The U.S. intelligence system puts a premium on quantity over quality, so that the good pieces get lost in the noise. There might be a better way of doing this but I haven't figured it out."[5] It is essential, however, that U.S. and other national intelligence agencies do figure out some way to utilize the best aspects of their proprietary intelligence. For, as Rwanda shows, it is wholly inadequate to rely on UN officials and reporters confined to the capital of a country, who may know little about the wider conflict or optimal intervention strategies.

Indeed, partly as a result of the media's failure to report the Rwandan genocide in a timely fashion, the media now suffers from exactly the opposite problem: the exaggeration of atrocities and premature characterization of civil violence as genocide. Rebels and human rights groups learned from Rwanda that they must declare "genocide" to have any hope of Western intervention. Because the press does not want to get caught napping again, it reports such claims even when it cannot confirm them. Accordingly, Western audiences were told that genocide was raging in Kosovo for months during 1999, but subsequent forensic investigation throughout the following year uncovered only about 3,000 corpses, some of whom appear to have been armed rebels. Likewise, Western media reported that genocide was occurring in East Timor after its September 1999 vote for independence, but five months later investigators had found only some 250 bodies.[6] A few hundred or thousand deaths are still significant, but they do not constitute genocide by any reasonable definition.

The media's failure to accurately report ethnic violence stems sometimes from intentional deception by at least one party to the conflict. For example, Rwanda's Hutu government wanted reporters to think that violence was civil war rather than genocide. Conversely, the Kosovo Liberation Army wanted reporters to think that violence carried out by the Yugoslav government before

NATO's bombing was genocide rather than counterinsurgency. In both cases, Western reporters were fooled. The decision whether to deploy intervention forces is too important for Western officials to make on the basis of such sketchy and manipulated information. This underscores the aforementioned need for better coordination of classified and nontraditional open-source information by national intelligence agencies.

The UN Secretariat also should enhance its coordination of available intelligence and the dissemination of that information to the Security Council as appropriate. However, it is inevitable that some individual states—including those contributing troops to a mission and those with vested interests in a region—will have access to classified intelligence that they will be reluctant to share with the United Nations for fear of endangering their troops or their intelligence-gathering sources and methods. The United Nations will not, and need not, have access to all such classified intelligence. The notion that failure to intervene quickly in Rwanda in 1994 can be attributed to inadequate UN intelligence gathering or distribution of that intelligence to member states is unsupportable. Belgium and at least three permanent members of the UN Security Council—the United States, France, and the United Kingdom—all knew promptly about the information in General Dallaire's January 1994 warning cable and consciously rejected the proposed response of reinforcing the UN peacekeepers already in Rwanda. There is no reason to believe that these key states would have made a different decision if the cable had received wider distribution among UN member states. Indeed, even after the genocide was in full swing and acknowledged by the UN secretary general, and an authorizing resolution had been passed by the UN Security Council, these key states still failed to provide troops and equipment in a timely manner.

Sixth, trade-offs are inevitable if the United States is to increase its effectiveness in humanitarian military intervention. As Rwanda highlights, quicker deployment can save more lives. However, U.S. troops currently are slow to deploy, despite enormous airlift resources, because their equipment, even in "light" units, is so heavy. Recent Pentagon initiatives to trim down some heavy mechanized forces into medium-weight units will not solve the problem, because they still will be too heavy for a quick airlift.[7] To routinely deploy troops faster, additional "ultra-light" units such as the 10th Mountain Division would have to be created, which would entail real costs. If such units were converted from existing heavier ones, the United States would be less prepared for more serious contingencies. Alternatively, if such units were added to the force structure, defense spending would increase. In either case, while such units probably could save more lives abroad, they also would be subject to more casualties and potential failure, as would any lighter force packages assembled today on an ad hoc basis. One key reason is that light units possess fewer organic transportation assets, so they are less mobile once on the ground, which impinges on mission effectiveness. Such potentially serious trade-offs should be made only after rigorous debate, which to date has been virtually absent in the United States.

Seventh, given that faster deployment can save more lives and that distant Africa has been the site of most large-scale ethnic violence in recent times, the effectiveness of intervention could be improved by prepositioning troops and equipment at African bases. Such forward deployment would permit interventions to rely on tactical airlifters, which are more widely available and more capable of landing at rudimentary African airfields than are strategic military aircraft. In addition, because flight distances from forward bases would be shorter and more theater airfields could be employed, each aircraft would be able to make one or more round-trip sorties to the theater per day, rather than one every four days from the United States. Shorter hops also would substantially reduce fuel requirements in the theater. The combination of these factors could potentially multiply a mission's daily cargo throughput severalfold, reducing total deployment time from weeks to days. These lessons are illustrated by the experience of the French military, which has repeatedly deployed relatively quickly from African bases to nearby states, including for Operation Turquoise to Rwanda, despite having a limited fleet of tactical airlifters and virtually no organic strategic airlift capacity. Although these past French interventions were too small and slow to prevent a raging genocide like that which occurred in Rwanda, they do demonstrate the advantages of forward positioning. Currently, the United States prepositions forces only in regions deemed vital to its national interest, such as Europe, East Asia, and the Persian Gulf—but not in Africa. Although the United States is willing to launch humanitarian interventions in certain cases after they become extremely violent and receive media attention, it apparently lacks sufficient will to make the advance investments necessary for such intervention to be more effective.

In recognition of the United States' lack of will to deploy its own ground troops to Africa, Washington launched a project called the African Crisis Response Initiative in the mid-1990s to create an indigenous all-African peacekeeping capability through training by the U.S. military. This initiative has a reasonable premise—that African states will be more willing than Western states to risk the lives of their troops to stop conflict on their own continent—but it has several shortcomings. First, to date all training has been nonlethal and therefore adequate only for peacekeeping in nonhostile environments as opposed to enforcement in situations of extreme violence. (Of course, there may be good reason for such restrictions because lethal training could be mis-used by a state to invade its neighbors or repress its people.) Second, the initiative so far has not prepositioned heavy weapons, armored personnel car-riers, or helicopters at African bases, so in the event of a crisis such equipment would have to be transported and married up to intervention forces on an ad hoc, protracted basis. Third, to date there has been only one training exercise at the brigade level, and most training has been conducted within national units at the battalion level or below, so even the trained forces are unprepared for large-scale coalition operations.[8] In light of these shortcomings, if another Rwanda-like genocide were to occur in Africa anytime soon, this all-African force would have little hope of mounting rapid or effective enforcement oper-ations to stop it.

An alternative proposal to facilitate rapid response was recently espoused in a UN report on improving peacekeeping by a panel chaired by Algerian diplomat Lakhdar Brahimi. The report, endorsed immediately by UN Secre-tary General Kofi Annan, recommended the expansion of UN standby arrangements "to include several coherent, multinational, brigade-size forces and the necessary enabling forces, created by Member States working in part-nership, in order to better meet the need for the robust peacekeeping forces that the Panel has advocated."[9] Although in theory such standby arrange-ments could enable faster interventions, there is ample reason for skepticism. For example, the report makes no provision for the coordination of airlift operations. Only the U.S. military has sufficient dedicated strategic airlift capacity to launch a rapid, large-scale deployment over a significant distance, which means that rapid reaction to most parts of the world is wishful thinking unless Washington participates. Even the European Union's proposed quick-reaction force, to be created by 2003, is being designed only to deploy itself within Europe. Thus what the Brahimi panel advocates as multilateral standby arrangements could in fact be held hostage to the consent of a single state.

Furthermore, even if UN member states were willing in the abstract to commit troops in advance to such standby arrangements, it is uncertain whether they would be willing actually to deploy them once the specifics of an intervention became clear. Indeed, it is not apparent that international rela-tions have changed much in this regard since the failure of the League of Nations' collective security system during the interwar period. As is well known, that failure resulted largely from the unrealistic expectation that states would be willing to sacrifice blood and treasure to intervene in conflicts in which they did not perceive a national interest, simply because they had com-mitted on paper to do so. Not only did league members fail to fulfill their commitments to respond to aggression by Nazi Germany, fascist Italy, and imperial Japan in the 1930s, but misplaced reliance on the League of Nations encouraged individual states to free-ride on the institution and therefore devote fewer of their own resources and less attention to maintaining international order, thereby contributing to the outbreak of World War II. In a similar way, the creation of standby arrangements for a UN rapid-reaction force could well reduce the willingness and preparedness of individual states for unilateral humanitarian intervention and thereby leave little back-up capability if the UN failed to mobilize its standby arrangements.

Eighth, there is an inherent tension between two main tenets of U.S. intervention policy—one that rejects the deployment of ground troops to ongoing civil wars, and another that favors intervention to prevent genocide. The reality is that the mass slaughter of civilians usually occurs in the context of civil war, where it is employed as a tactic by one or both sides. To prevent such killing, ground intervention forces would have to be deployed to ongoing civil wars before evidence of genocide became clear. Thus U.S. national security officials must confront the hard question of which of these two principles is more important, because in many cases they will be mutually incompatible. In any case, the nation's peacekeeping policy, codified in Presidential Decision Directive 25, should be modified to eliminate the provisions that compelled the United States to block Belgium's request for UN authorization to reinforce UNAMIR with non-U.S. troops two months before the genocide. Washington's lack of will to deploy its own ground troops to prevent conflict in obscure parts of the world does not justify its preventing other good samaritans from trying to do so.

Ninth, experiences in the 1990s demonstrated that although the international community has sufficient will to intervene in many conflicts, it rarely has sufficient will to devote the resources necessary to intervene effectively. In Rwanda, as in Bosnia's "safe area" of Srebrenica, the international community deployed a small peacekeeping force that was unable to defend itself, let alone vulnerable civilians. When killers went on the rampage, peacekeepers had little choice but to stand aside. Despite these shameful and embarrassing incidents, and the media exposés and UN mea culpas that followed them, some intervention advocates in the U.S. government and at the United Nations continue to promote the deployment of small peacekeeping forces to high-risk situations of unresolved civil war. The most recent case is that of the Democratic Republic of Congo (former Zaire), where the United Nations has proposed to deploy 5,000 peacekeepers to a country with a population of at least 50 million, on the basis of a peace agreement known as the Lusaka Accords, which the parties signed under coercion and originally had little intention of honoring. (Prospects for peace now appear improved because of the assassination of Congo's intransigent president, Laurent Kabila, in January 2001 and the succession of his more conciliatory son, Joseph. Still, peace depends mainly on the political will of the parties to the conflict—rather than on a handful of peacekeepers dispersed to a few locations in this enormous country and authorized primarily to defend themselves.)

Supporters of such feeble deployments argue that there is nothing to lose: if the peacekeepers help to foster a climate of trust, they can contribute to building peace; if they prove inadequate and war resumes, they have not hurt the situation. But such analyses are short-sighted for several reasons. First, every time peacekeepers withdraw in the midst of a bloodbath the overall credibility of humanitarian intervention is further undermined, which makes the international community less likely to provide future financial and human resources to peacekeeping missions, even those that are worthwhile and well designed. In addition, withdrawing under fire in one case encourages spoilers in other civil-war peace processes to attack peacekeepers in order to spur their withdrawal as well. Moreover, the deployment of even a small group of peace-keepers changes the dynamics of a conflict and raises expectations among the local parties that they will be afforded at least some degree of protection. This false sense of security can encourage one or more of the parties to let down their guard, thereby increasing their vulnerability. If violence then resumes and peacekeepers are helpless to stop it, as in Rwanda in 1994 or Angola in 1992, even more innocent civilians may die than would have if the peacekeepers had not been deployed in the first place. In other words, halfway measures such as deploying inadequately sized intervention forces—or adequate forces with inadequate mandates—to high-risk peacekeeping situations may be worse than doing nothing. The perceived imperative to "do something," in the absence of sufficient will to do the right thing, may ultimately increase the number of victims.

Finally, no policy of humanitarian military intervention should be implemented without a sober assessment of another of its unintended consequences, that arising from "moral hazard." Recent interventions—whether in Bosnia, Kosovo, or East Timor—have been motivated by the impulse to provide humanitarian aid to a party visibly suffering in an internal conflict. However, such intervention also has resulted in the weaker side being bolstered militarily. This pattern creates perverse incentives for weaker parties in such conflicts to escalate the fighting and thereby exacerbate the suffering of their own people, because they expect or hope to attract foreign intervention. Thus, a policy of intervening to relieve humanitarian emergencies that stem from internal conflicts may unintentionally increase the number and extent of such emergencies—a classic instance of moral hazard.[10]

Of course, most members of the victim group in such cases do not willingly invite their fate. But the leaders of these groups do sometimes provoke retaliation against their own civilians in order to galvanize domestic and, especially, international support. The Bosnian government repeatededly used this tactic in its 1992–95 war, as was documented by at least two UN commanders on the ground.[11] More recently, this cynical tactic was copied with even greater success by the Kosovo Liberation Army. As long as the West comes to the military assistance of groups being victimized because of their own violent provocations, it risks fostering an escalation of ethnic conflict.

This is not to say that the moral hazard dynamic is responsible for the escalation of all or even most civil wars. Indeed, it was not a major factor for most of the Rwandan civil war. However, during 1993–94 international pressure on the Habyarimana government and the deployment of UN peacekeepers did foster the RPF's uncompromising brinkmanship in demanding a negotiated handover of power, which contributed to the outbreak and extent of the genocide. Even more clearly, in several other cases including Bosnia and Kosovo, the expectation of humanitarian intervention demonstrably contributed to the escalation of conflict and retaliatory atrocities. Given that each instance of humanitarian intervention can raise future expectations of such intervention, the resulting moral hazard must be counted as a cost of this type of action. Although intervention may still be the right choice in a specific case if this cost and others are outweighed by the expected benefits, the associated increase in moral hazard is nonetheless a cost that should not be ignored.

Some have suggested that the moral-hazard problem could be eliminated if the international community were to commit to intervene promptly in every case of humanitarian atrocities. In practice, however, this would mean that Western militaries would have to prevent retaliation against every group that chose unilaterally to rebel, secede, or revolt. Given the large numbers of existing civil wars, and the extra ones that would be spurred by the announcement of such a policy, it is obvious that honoring such a commitment in even a fraction of cases would be well beyond the means and will of the international community. Unfortunately, risks stemming from the moral hazard associated with humanitarian intervention cannot be eliminated. They can only be managed—and even then only after statesmen acknowledge them, which to date they have been reluctant to do.

In summary, despite preventive efforts by the international community— or in some cases because of such efforts—certain states will continue to suffer internal conflicts that put them at high risk of civil war and accompanying civilian atrocities. In each case, the United States and the international community will have four options as to when to intervene militarily: before the outbreak or renewal of civil war; immediately upon the outbreak of civil war; only after civil war leads to genocide; or not at all. Preventive intervention with a substantial force before the outbreak of full-blown war probably would save the most lives and is especially feasible in cases where the host government invites in peacekeepers, but it could soon exhaust Western resources if exercised frequently. Intervening after the outbreak of war by deploying a large ground force might avert genocide in some cases but would raise the risks of incurring casualties and becoming caught in quagmires that could undercut support for continued humanitarian intervention, and also might quickly exhaust Western resources if commonly practiced. Deploying troops immediately upon identification of genocide could reduce the toll of such killing, but where violence was being perpetrated rapidly, as in Rwanda, troops could not arrive in time to save most of the intended victims. Eschewing military intervention completely would allow certain civil wars and genocides to rage on with mounting casualties, but might avert this type of violence elsewhere by discouraging weak groups from escalating conflicts in the expectation of attracting Western intervention.

Clearly, none of these options can be relied on to avert genocide in every case. Moreover, decisions about whether and how to intervene in specific cases inevitably will be caught up in politics. However, for such decisions to have a good chance of success they must be informed by realistic appraisals of the prospects of humanitarian intervention rather than wishful thinking about the ease of saving lives with force.

APPENDIX A

A Model of the
Genocide's Progression

THE SIMPLIFYING ASSUMPTIONS that follow undergird this book's model of the quantitative progression of the genocide. They are based on the geographic progression of the genocide as described in the text:

1. In five prefectures where virtually all large massacres took place by April 21, 1994—Cyangugu, Gikongoro, Kibungo, Kibuye, and Kigali—it is assumed that 50 percent of the Tutsi were killed by that date. Subsequently in these prefectures, 10 percent of the remaining Tutsi are estimated to have been killed weekly for as long as the genocide continued there. During the first week, it is estimated that 15 percent of Tutsi died in the first four prefectures listed, but 25 percent in Kigali prefecture—which includes the capital, where killing started more rapidly.

2. Because the genocide in Butare prefecture started late but then commenced with a vengeance, it is estimated that no Tutsi were killed during the first week but that 40 percent of the Tutsi there were killed by April 21, 1994, and thereafter 10 percent weekly of those remaining for as long as the genocide continued there.

3. Because there were very few large massacres in Gisenyi and Ruhengeri, the 10 percent weekly figure is used for the course of the genocide there. This

120

Table A-1. *Tutsi Population by Prefecture on the Eve of Genocide*[a]

Prefecture	1991			1994
	Total population of Rwanda	Tutsi population	Tutsi by prefecture (percent)	Tutsi population[b]
Butare	764,795	128,145	16.76	140,960
Byumba	779,665	10,805	1.39	11,886
Cyangugu	517,135	55,345	10.70	60,880
Gikongoro	466,290	58,155	12.47	63,971
Gisenyi	729,855	21,730	2.98	23,903
Gitarama	851,145	78,405	9.21	86,146
Kibungo	646,555	44,405	6.87	48,846
Kibuye	473,920	71,225	15.03	78,348
Kigali (w/ city)	1,150,740	118,980	10.34	130,878
Ruhengeri	769,115	3,705	0.48	4,076
All Rwanda	7,149,215	590,900	8.27	649,990

Source: 1991 figures: *Recensement Général de la Population et de l'Habitat au 15 Aout 1991, Résultats Préliminaires Echantillon au 10e* (Kigali: Service National de Recensement, République Rwandaise, December 1992), p. 23, table 5.

a. Numbers extrapolated from 1991 census figures.

b. Tutsi population of 1994 is estimated and assumes 10 percent growth from 1991.

is probably an underestimate of the rate of killing, but the actual number of Tutsi in the two prefectures at the start of genocide was probably significantly smaller than indicated by the 1991 census because of the ethnic cleansing that had occurred before the genocide. These effects should tend to cancel each other out and provide a rough estimate of the number of Tutsi killed. In any case, the number of Tutsi in the two prefectures is so small that the country-wide results should not be significantly biased.

4. Because the genocide started late in Gitarama and proceeded gradually thereafter, no Tutsi are estimated to have been killed during the first two weeks of genocide, and 10 percent weekly subsequently until the genocide ended there.

5. Because the RPF controlled much of Byumba before the outbreak of genocide, and the remainder of the prefecture shortly thereafter, the model makes the simplifying assumption that no Tutsi there were killed. In reality, some were killed there. In addition, some of Byumba's Tutsi population had fled the prefecture more than a year before the genocide in response to the RPF's occupation in early 1993 and had not returned before the genocide, so they likely were killed elsewhere.[1]

6. In the three prefectures of Operation Turquoise, the arrival of French troops in late June is estimated to have reduced the Tutsi death rate by half, to

Table A-2. *Estimated Rwandan Tutsi Survivors of Genocide by Prefecture and Week, 1994*

Date	Butare	Byumba	Cyangugu	Gikongoro	Gisenyi	Gitarama	Kibungo	Kibuye	Kigali	Ruhengeri	Total	Percent
April 7	140,960	11,886	60,880	63,971	23,903	86,246	48,846	78,348	130,878	4,076	649,990	100.0
April 14	140,960	11,886	51,748	54,375	21,513	86,246	41,519	66,595	98,159	3,668	576,667	88.7
April 21	84,576	11,886	30,440	31,985	19,361	86,246	24,423	39,174	65,439	3,301	396,830	61.1
April 28	76,118	11,886	27,396	28,787	17,425	77,621	21,980	35,256	58,895	2,971	358,336	55.1
May 5	68,506	11,886	24,656	25,908	15,683	69,859	21,980	31,731	53,006	2,674	325,889	50.1
May 12	61,656	11,886	22,191	23,317	14,114	62,873	21,980	28,558	47,705	2,407	296,687	45.6
May 19	55,490	11,886	19,972	20,986	12,703	56,586	21,980	25,702	42,935	2,166	270,404	41.6
May 26	49,941	11,886	17,974	18,887	11,433	50,927	21,980	23,132	38,641	1,949	246,751	38.0
June 2	44,947	11,886	16,177	16,998	10,289	45,835	21,980	20,819	34,777	1,754	225,462	34.7
June 9	40,452	11,886	14,559	15,298	9,261	41,251	21,980	18,737	31,299	1,579	206,303	31.7
June 16	36,407	11,886	13,103	13,769	8,334	37,126	21,980	16,863	28,169	1,421	189,059	29.1
June 23	32,766	11,886	11,793	12,392	7,501	37,126	21,980	15,177	25,352	1,279	177,252	27.3
June 30	29,490	11,886	11,203	11,772	6,751	37,126	21,980	14,418	22,817	1,151	168,594	25.9
July 7	26,541	11,886	10,643	11,184	6,076	37,126	21,980	13,697	20,535	1,036	160,704	24.7
July 14	26,541	11,886	10,111	10,624	5,468	37,126	21,980	13,012	20,535	932	158,216	24.3
July 21	26,541	11,886	9,605	10,093	4,921	37,126	21,980	12,362	20,535	932	155,982	24.0

Source: For assumptions of this chart, see text in appendix A.

5 percent weekly, before halting killing in late July. The French assert that the killing ended in late June.[2]

7. As prefectures were captured by the RPA during the renewed civil war, the genocide is estimated to have halted there immediately, even though it is known to have continued in isolated pockets for a brief period.

8. The model's estimates of the number of Tutsi from each prefecture who survived the genocide does not imply that those survivors remained in their home prefecture throughout the genocide. Indeed, many survived by becoming refugees or fleeing to RPF zones. Thus, the number of survivors from a prefecture according to the model need not match the number actually found in that prefecture after the genocide.

Airlift in Some Previous
U.S. Military Interventions

F OUR PREVIOUS U.S. airborne interventions were expedited by factors that would have been absent in Rwanda. Nevertheless, these cases provide useful insights into some of the constraining variables in airlift operations. The following capsule descriptions serve as background to the summary data contained in table 7-1.

LEBANON, 1958. The airlift of army troops to Lebanon in 1958, for Operation Blue Bat, was facilitated by several factors: a few days' advance warning, which enabled the preparation and loading of cargo; a large staging base in Adana, Turkey, that held up to 147 fixed-wing aircraft on the ground at one time; and the presence of suitable U.S. troops already in Europe, only 2,500 miles away from the theater.[1] Still, the operation was hindered by perennial obstacles, including poor planning and a lack of unloading equipment in the staging and theater air bases, so that much of the cargo had to be unloaded by hand.[2] As a result, on average, only about 400 tons and 500 personnel per day could be airlifted during the first week.[3]

DOMINICAN REPUBLIC, 1965. The deployment to the Dominican Republic in 1965, Operation Power Pack, was much more impressive in its airlift of men and materiel, averaging 2,000 tons and 2,300 troops per day during the first week.[4] In addition, the army was resupplied exclusively by air for the first eleven days of the operation.[5] These achievements were made possible by the proximity of the theater, a mere 1,200 miles from the U.S. Army's 82d Airborne Division, based at Fort Bragg, N.C., adjacent to Pope Air Force Base. This short distance enabled reliance on 204 tactical C-130 aircraft, which ordinarily cannot take part in strategic lifts because they cannot refuel in the air, in addition to ninety C-124 and nineteen C-119 older tactical lifters.[6] The airlift also benefited from the proximity of Ramey Air Force Base in neighboring Puerto Rico, to relieve overloading of the Dominican airhead at San Isidro. As a result of these advantages, the round trip from U.S. bases could be accomplished in less than twenty-four hours, several times faster than for a strategic airlift to Africa.[7]

GRENADA, 1983. The deployment to Grenada in 1983, Operation Urgent Fury, included a three-day airlift operation that similarly transported 2,000 troops per day. This speed was made possible by several factors: a week's advance notification; predeployment of some troops to Barbados a day before the invasion; a light cargo load due to the absence in the airlift of any combat vehicles, which instead were sealifted and brought ashore by marines in an amphibious landing; and again the very short distance from U.S. bases.[8] Airlifted troops were drawn mainly from the 82d Airborne Division in North Carolina, air assets from the 101st Air Assault Division in Kentucky, and U.S. Army Rangers (which seized the airhead) from Georgia. All were within 2,000 miles of Grenada.[9]

PANAMA, 1989. The deployment to Panama in 1989, Operation Just Cause, was eased by the presence there of a U.S. military base with 13,000 American troops, already outfitted with equipment and logistics, which significantly reduced lift requirements. The airlift was also facilitated by the relative proximity of the theater to continental U.S. bases only 1,500 to 3,500 miles away. During the first week, an average of about 500 tons of cargo and 900 troops per day were airlifted, using twelve C-5, seventy-seven C-141, and twenty-two C-130 aircraft, in addition to 176 helicopters.[10] During the second week, airlift increased significantly to an average of 1,100 tons and 500 troops per day, for a two-week total of 11,700 tons of cargo and 9,500 troops.[11] On the third day of the intervention, in response to widespread looting and arson in Panama City, 3,000 American troops were designated for policing, a troop presence representing seven per thousand of the city's population. (If the capital's suburban population is included, the policing ratio was only four per thousand.)[12]

Theater Airfield Capacity
Based on Operation
Support Hope

THE EXPERIENCE OF Operation Support Hope, the U.S. humanitarian relief mission immediately following the genocide, best indicates the capacity of central African airfields for an earlier hypothetical airborne intervention to stop the genocide. Information is publicly available on the daily cargo flows and number of U.S. sorties into the three main theater airfields in Operation Support Hope—Goma, Zaire; Kigali, Rwanda; and Entebbe, Uganda. Data on the number of NGO flights are lacking. However, the available information is sufficient to estimate the maximum sustainable cargo throughput at each of these airfields, which likely would have served as the backbone of any earlier airborne intervention to stop the genocide. In all cases, the maximum *sustainable* daily throughput at an airfield is lower than the single-day maximum experienced during the operation. This is because single-day maximums are achieved by overloading an airfield, which inevitably reduces capacity during the following days because the airfield's ramp space is clogged with aircraft unloading and being serviced. Thus a better gauge is the daily average achieved during busy stints of several consecutive days.

At the rudimentary airfield in Goma, Zaire, the maximum number of sorties reported in a single day during Operation Support Hope was twenty-one, but these were mainly smaller-capacity tactical aircraft, which require less ramp space and servicing and carried a total cargo of only 115 tons. The maximum cargo throughput in a single day at Goma was 273 tons carried by eleven sorties. The maximum number of strategic U.S. sorties over a two-day period was fifteen, at a time when there were very few or no additional NGO flights. Thus the airfield probably could sustain an average of about six strategic sorties daily. Assuming a realistic mix of 4 C-141 and 2 C-5 sorties per day, this would translate into a maximum sustainable cargo throughput of about 200 tons daily. If the airfield served mainly to handle tactical sorties, as is likely, its capacity probably would be somewhat lower.[1]

At Kigali airport, the maximum one-day throughput was 526 tons. In addition, during a particularly busy four-day stretch, the airport handled thirty-three strategic and twenty-six tactical U.S. sorties, possibly in addition to a few NGO flights, a daily average of at least eight strategic and six tactical sorties. Assuming a realistic capacity of five C-141, three C-5, and six C-130 aircraft per day, the airport would have a maximum sustainable cargo throughput of approximately 400 tons daily.[2]

At Entebbe airport, cargo levels were not reported, but the number of U.S. sorties were. During a three-day peak of activity, the airport handled thirty-eight strategic and thirty-one tactical U.S. sorties, possibly in addition to NGO flights. The strategic sorties are most relevant for determining the airfield's receiving capacity, because the tactical sorties carried transloaded cargo *away* from Entebbe, as they would have if an earlier airborne intervention had been launched to stop the genocide.[3] Assuming a sustainable daily flow of a dozen strategic sorties, and a realistic mix of eight C-141 and four C-5 aircraft with realistic payloads, this airfield also had the capacity to receive about 400 tons daily.[4]

In addition, there are several small regional airfields located in Rwanda. Another such airfield is located just across the Western border in Bukavu, Congo (Zaire), which received some use during both Operation Support Hope and France's earlier Operation Turquoise. However, these small airfields have limited ramp space and short rudimentary runways that could not have accommodated the U.S. strategic aircraft available in 1994. Accordingly, these airfields would have had less capacity even than Goma and would not have been relied on routinely for an intervention to stop the genocide. In an emergency, each could have handled perhaps a dozen tactical sorties daily, carrying up to a thousand troops or 100 tons of cargo, but only for a brief period because the repeated landings and take-offs would have degraded their landing strips. As the commander of Operation Support Hope noted during the

operation: "Airlift into Bukavu is not a viable option for the size of the requirement. . . . Given the runway surface and composition, the Bukavu airstrip will
not be usable much longer than 10-14 days if air traffic exceeds the present rate
of 3-4 C-130 [tactical] sorties and grows to 10-15 daily. Repair or reconstruc-
tion of the strip would require its closure and complete resurfacing."[5]
Nominally, fifteen C-130 sorties could carry about 300 tons of cargo, but none
of these smaller airports had the off-loading capacity to handle such a daily
throughput.[6]

During Operation Support Hope, the maximum throughput at each of
the three main airfields was attained only gradually as improvements were
made to runways, air traffic control, fuel supplies, and facilities. Goma and
Entebbe ramped up relatively quickly, because they recently had been
upgraded for the airlift of France's Operation Turquoise. At Entebbe both the
French and American operations also benefited from using the defunct airport
(of Israeli commando fame) adjacent to the current airport for additional
ramp space. In addition, the ramp-up of Operation Support Hope was facilitated by previous U.S. Air Force familiarity with Entebbe that was gained
during ninety-one sorties to the region carrying 1,788 tons of cargo in support
of the French-led operation. At Goma, even with the improvements provided
by Operation Turquoise, airfield conditions were hazardous, especially for
strategic aircraft. Accordingly, Operation Support Hope usually relied on
transloading cargo elsewhere from strategic to tactical aircraft for the lift to
Goma, except during the first three days of August 1994. At Kigali airport,
throughput capacity was slower to expand because the airfield had suffered
significant damage as a prime battleground in the renewed civil war and therefore had lost its certification from the U.S. Federal Aviation Administration,
which ordinarily is required for landings by strategic aircraft, though not tactical sorties. U.S. Air Force personnel arrived at the airport on July 29, 1994,
and managed to open it for twenty-four-hour operations within one day.
However, the airfield received a total of only eight sorties (two strategic, six tactical) over its first four days of operation through August 1. Had the United
States launched an airborne intervention during the first weeks of the genocide, Goma and Entebbe would have ramped up more slowly than they did in
Operation Support Hope because they would not yet have benefited from the
experience of Operation Turquoise. However, Kigali would have ramped up
faster because it would not yet have been so damaged by the war. Accordingly,
the overall theater airfield capacity in an earlier intervention to stop the genocide would have expanded at approximately the same rate as in Operation
Support Hope.[7]

Notes

Preface

1. Alan J. Kuperman, "False Hope Abroad: Promises to Intervene Often Bring Bloodshed," *Washington Post*, June 14, 1998, Outlook Secttion; Alan J. Kuperman, "Transnational Causes of Genocide, or How the West Inadvertently Exacerbates Ethnic Conflict in the Post–Cold War Era," presented at the annual meeting of the American Political Science Association, Atlanta, Ga., September 2–5, 1999.

Chapter One

1. See Ivo H. Daalder, "Knowing When to Say No: The Development of U.S. Policy for Peacekeeping," in William Durch, ed., *UN Peacekeeping, American Politics, and the Uncivil Wars of the 1990s* (New York: St. Martin's, 1996).

2. Charles Krauthammer, *Washington Post*, December 11, 1992; Yael S. Aronoff, "Clinton's Rwanda Apology Is Fine, but America Needs to Act," *Washington Post*, April 10, 1998; Holly Burkhalter, Physicians for Human Rights, "The 1994 Rwandan Genocide and U.S. Policy," testimony before the House Subcommittee on Human Rights and International Operations, May 5, 1998; Henry Kissinger quoted in *Charlie Rose Show*, Transcript 2140, April 16, 1998; Michael Kelly, "A Perfectly Clintonian Doctrine," *Washington Post*, June 30, 1999; Jim Hoagland, "Kosovos to Come," *Washington Post*, June 27, 1999.

3. For example, in response to a question about the Rwandan genocide during the second presidential debate, Bush stated, "That's a case where we need to . . . use our influence to have countries in Africa come together and help deal with the situation. The [Clinton] administration . . . made the right decision on training Nigerian troops for situations just such as this in Rwanda." Transcript, second presidential debate of 2000, Wake Forest University, Winston-Salem, N.C., October 11, 2000 (www.cnn.com/ELECTION/2000/debates/transcripts/u221011.html [November 13, 2000]).

4. There are at least a couple of important exceptions. See, for example, Barry Posen, "Military Responses to Refugee Disasters," *International Security*, vol. 21 (Summer 1996), pp. 72–111; and Michael O'Hanlon, *Saving Lives with Force: Military*

Criteria for Humanitarian Intervention (Brookings Institution, 1997). However, O'Hanlon's assumptions about quickly transporting well-equipped troops to a distant theater are overly optimistic and not empirically based.

5. James Fearon, "Counterfactuals and Hypothesis Testing in Political Science," *World Politics*, vol. 43 (January 1991), pp. 169ff.

6. See, for example, Scott R. Feil, *Preventing Genocide: How the Early Use of Force Might Have Succeeded in Rwanda* (New York: Carnegie Corporation of New York, 1998). See also Col. Scott R. Feil, "Could 5,000 Peacekeepers Have Saved 500,000 Rwandans? Early Intervention Reconsidered," *ISD Reports*, Georgetown University Institute for the Study of Diplomacy, vol. 3 (April 1997).

Chapter Two

1. For further detail on the background to the genocide, see Alan J. Kuperman, "The Other Lesson of Rwanda: Mediators Sometimes Do More Damage Than Good," *SAIS Review*, vol. 16 (Winter–Spring 1996): 221–40. This chapter also draws from longer histories, including Dixon Kamukama, *Rwanda Conflict: Its Roots and Regional Implications* (Kampala, Uganda: Fountain, 1993); Gérard Prunier, *The Rwanda Crisis: History of a Genocide* (New York: Columbia University Press, 1995); Filip Reyntjens, *L'Afrique des Grands Lacs en Crise: Rwanda, Burundi, 1988–1994* (Paris: Karthala, 1994); Ntaribi Kamanzi, *Rwanda: Du Génocide a la Défaite* (Kigali: Editions Rebero, 1997).

2. For more on this debate, see "Crisis in Central Africa: The History of Politics and the Politics of History," *Africa Today*, vol. 45 (January–March 1998),

3. For citations, please refer to the more detailed discussion below regarding estimates of the number of Tutsi killed in the genocide.

4. Reyntjens, *L'Afrique des Grands Lacs en Crise*, pp. 34–35.

5. See Alain Rouvez, with the assistance of Michael Coco and Jean-Paul Paddack, *Disconsolate Empires: French, British, and Belgian Military Involvement in Post-Colonial Sub-Saharan Africa* (Lanham, Md.: University Press of America, 1994), pp. 186, 342–45.

6. RPF officials, interviews with author, Kigali, Rwanda, April 1999.

7. Kamanzi, *Rwanda*, pp. 53ff, provides an excellent account of Habyarimana's successful efforts to co-opt the Hutu opposition. Only the Parti Social Démocrate (PSD) did not form a Hutu Power faction and, as a result, virtually its entire leadership was killed at the start of the genocide.

8. Filip Reyntjens argues that the RPF shares blame for this delay in implementation, apparently because it refused to compromise and would not accept any deviations from the Arusha structure or the candidate lists submitted by the pro-rebel factions of the opposition parties. However, because it was Habyarimana who insisted on modifying the terms of a signed agreement and who fostered schisms within the opposition parties in order to obstruct its implementation, he must be assigned the bulk of

responsibility for the delay. Filip Reyntjens, *Rwanda: Trois jours qui ont fait basculer l'histoire* (Paris: Editions L'Harmattan, 1995), p. 17; and e-mail communication to author, September 27, 1999.

Chapter Three

1. African Rights, *Rwanda: Death, Despair and Defiance*, rev. ed. (London: African Rights, August 1995). It should be noted that Filip Reyntjens criticizes African Rights as "flagrantly pro-RPF, which is incompatible with the mission and ethics of all serious human rights organizations" (Filip Reyntjens, *Rwanda: Trois jours qui ont fait basculer l'histoire* (Paris: Editions L'Harmattan, 1995), p. 62), author's translation.

2. Alison Des Forges, *Leave None to Tell the Story: Genocide in Rwanda* (New York: Human Rights Watch, 1999).

3. Ibid., p. 16.

4. Concentrating a dispersed populace is an essential step in modern genocides that is usually orchestrated by the killers. The fact that Tutsi in Rwanda self-congregated rapidly saved the extremists a step and may explain the unprecedented speed of the genocide. I am grateful to Benjamin Valentino for this observation. Des Forges (*Leave None*, pp. 209–10) confirms that Tutsi initially self-congregated. Beginning April 11, the government helped facilitate the process by promising falsely to protect Tutsi if they would assemble at large central sites.

5. African Rights, *Rwanda: Death, Despair*, p. 259.

6. Des Forges (*Leave None*, pp. 8, 211) concurs that soldiers and national police led all the major massacres while local administrators organized the rousting of Tutsi from their homes and the concentration of Tutsi at central sites. She dates the start of large-scale massacres to April 11, 1994. Kamanzi notes that many Hutu as well sought protection at the central sites in the chaos of the first days of violence; see Ntaribi Kamanzi, *Rwanda: Du Génocide a la Défaite* (Kigali: Editions Rebero, 1997), pp. 103–05. These Hutu generally were instructed by authorities to leave before the sites were sacked. He reports that "the weekend of April 9–10, 1994 was one of the bloodiest in the history of the genocide, especially in Kigali and Kibungo," in southeastern Rwanda. In Kigali, political assassinations were carried out by the Presidential Guard, who were guided to their targets by the militias (author's translation).

7. In one exceptional instance in the parish of Nyange in Kibuye prefecture on April 15, 1994, bulldozers were used to collapse a church's walls on top of 2,000 Tutsi. See African Rights, *Rwanda: Death, Despair*, pp. 402–16.

8. African Rights (ibid., p. 258), says that most Tutsi were killed at such sites. Alison Des Forges estimates that roughly half were killed at them, although she says the true figure is uncertain and could equally be 40 percent or 60 percent (personal communication, August 22, 1998).

9. Des Forges concurs: "By two weeks into the campaign, they had slain hundreds of thousands of Tutsi" (*Leave None*, p. 770).

10. Alison Des Forges, e-mail communication to author, December 21, 1997. Des Forges (*Leave None*, pp. 630, 634) confirms that the presence of foreigners deterred massacres.

11. African Rights, *Rwanda: Death, Despair*, pp. 686–747.

12. Ibid.

13. At the time of the 1991 census, Rwanda had ten prefectures. In 1992, Kigali prefecture was split into an urban and a rural prefecture, so there were officially eleven prefectures at the time of the genocide. In 1996 the former hunting area of Mutara in northeastern Rwanda was split off from Byumba as a twelfth prefecture. For consistency, this book refers to the ten prefectures extant in 1991.

14. African Rights reports that in Butare prefecture 20,000 were killed on April 19 at a church in Cyahinda, and 40,000 the next day at a church in Karama, although these figures may be exaggerated (see African Rights, *Rwanda: Death, Despair*, pp. 337–45).

15. See Commission d'enquête parlementaire concernant les événements du Rwanda, *Rapport* (Brussels: Senat de Belgique, December 6, 1997), testimony of M. Degni-Segui, former UN special rapporteur for Rwanda, section 3.6.4.1, author's translations (www.senate.be/docs), hereafter cited as *Belgian Senate Report*. See also Des Forges, *Leave None*, pp. 263, 270–72, which confirms that there were relatively few killings in Butare and Gitarama until near the end of the second week.

16. Des Forges, *Leave None*, pp. 23, 699–700.

17. Ibid., p. 283.

18. Author's interview with RPF officials, Kigali, April 1999.

19. Bernard Lugan, *Histoire du Rwanda* (Etrepilly, France: Bartillat, 1997), pp. 516–17; *Belgian Senate Report*, section 3.6.3.

20. Reyntjens, *Rwanda: Trois jours*, pp. 82–83.

21. Gérard Prunier, *The Rwanda Crisis: History of a Genocide* (New York: Columbia University Press, 1995), p. 264.

22. The source for the 1956 census figures is Filip Reyntjens, fax to author, November 3, 1998. The Hutu were counted as 82.74 percent and Twa as 0.67 percent.

23. Catharine Watson estimates that the true percentage of Tutsi immediately before independence was 14 percent, of which some 40 to 70 percent—150,000 to 250,000—fled between 1959 and 1964 (see Catharine Watson, *Exile from Rwanda: Background to an Invasion*, U.S. Committee for Refugees, February 1991, p. 6). If those figures are correct, only 4.7 to 8.9 percent of Rwanda's population after the initial exodus would have been Tutsi, an even smaller percentage than the government census produced. Any estimate of the Tutsi percentage of the population after the revolutionary violence is sensitive to the number of Tutsi who actually fled in the exodus from 1959 to 1964, which has never been determined with precision. The analysis in the text relies on an oft-cited, mid-range estimate of 200,000.

24. Des Forges, *Leave None*, p. 15.

25. Des Forges (ibid., p. 15), reports 150,000 Tutsi survivors, which is 20,000 more than earlier reported by Prunier (*The Rwanda Crisis*, p. 265). The estimated number

of Tutsi survivors could be an undercount if some surviving Tutsi avoided the tally, or an overcount if some surviving Hutu, to avoid retribution after the genocide, succeeded in passing as Tutsi, thereby artificially inflating the survivor figures. Rwanda conducted a new "genocide victims' census" from July 17 to 27, 2000, which could help shed light on the actual number of victims and survivors of the genocide, but at this writing the results had not been released. See "Rwanda: Results of Genocide Census Delayed," UN Integrated Regional Information Network for Central and Eastern Africa, July 31, 2000.

26. A demographer consulted by Human Rights Watch likewise estimated there were only 657,000 Tutsi in Rwanda immediately before the genocide. She also estimated that three-quarters of the Tutsi were killed (Des Forges, *Leave None*, pp. 15, 27). Filip Reyntjens agrees that the government census figures are fairly accurate, although he estimates that the pregenocide Tutsi proportion may have been as high as 10 percent, or nearly 800,000 Tutsi (fax communication to author, August 7, 1998).

27. See Filip Reyntjens, "Estimation du Nombre de Personnes Tuées au Rwanda en 1994," in S. Marysse and F. Reyntjens, *L'Afrique des Grands Lacs: Annuaire 1996–1997* (Paris: Editions L'Harmattan, 1997), pp. 179–86; Filip Reyntjens, e-mail communication to author, September 1, 1998; *Belgian Senate Report*, section 3.6.1, citing Prunier; Des Forges, *Leave None*, pp. 16, 724, 726, 730–31.

Chapter Four

1. Former senior officials at the Pentagon, State Department, and National Security Council who had responsibility for Rwanda during the genocide, interviews with author.

2. Linda Melvern reports that during the first week of violence U.S. Senator Paul Simon did speak to General Roméo Dallaire and then called the White House to convey his concerns (see Linda Melvern, "Genocide behind the Thin Blue Line," *Security Dialogue*, vol. 28 [September 1997], pp. 340–41). However, Dallaire was unaware of the scope of killing at the time and concerned mainly about renewed civil war, so Simon presumably did not warn the White House of genocide.

3. The existence of only a single U.S. human intelligence asset in the entire region is confirmed by three former Pentagon officials, in separate interviews with author.

4. Former NSC official, interviews with author, January 23, 2001, and February 20, 2001.

5. "Carnage in Africa," *The Times*, April 11, 1994; Axel Buyse, "Chaos in Rwanda Threatens Stability of Whole Region," *De Standaard*, April 12, 1994, p. 3, in FBIS-AFR-94-072, April 14, 1994; Jeff Drumtra, "Rwanda: Genocide and the Continuing Cycle of Violence," testimony of the U.S. Committee for Refugees before the House International Relations Committee, May 5, 1998, p. 4; "UN in Rwanda Says It Is Powerless to Halt the Violence," *New York Times*, April 15, 1994, p. 3; Mark Huband, "UN Troops Seek Ceasefire in Blood-Soaked Rwanda," *Guardian*, April 15, 1994, emphasis added;

"Des Parachutistes français prennent position sur l'aéroport de Kigali," *Le Monde*, April 10–11, 1994; "Le Rwanda à feu et à sang," *Le Monde*, April 12, 1994, p. 1; Alison Des Forges, e-mail communication to author, December 21, 1997. Filip Reyntjens contends that almost as many Hutu as Tutsi ultimately died in the violence; see Reyntjens, "Estimation du Nombre de Personnes Tuées au Rwanda en 1994," in S. Marysse and F. Reyntjens, *L'Afrique des Grands Lacs: Annuaire 1996–1997* (Paris: Editions L'Harmattan, 1997), pp. 179–86. If this is true, it means the killing was mutual, at least over time, although Reyntjens never characterizes it as such.

6. (Clandestine) Radio Muhabura, 1900 GMT, April 18, 1994, in FBIS-AFR-94-076, April 20, 1994, p. 5.

7. Alison Des Forges, *Leave None to Tell the Story: Genocide in Rwanda* (New York: Human Rights Watch, 1999), pp. 255, 623, 709, 712–13.

8. Paris Radio France International, April 11, 1994, 1230 GMT, in FBIS-AFR-94-070, April 12, 1994, p. 1; "Rwanda: la capitale livrée à elle-même," *Le Monde*, April 13, 1994. The rebels said they were willing to accept only a cease-fire limited to the capital ("Cabinet Flees Kigali as Army Resists Rebel Push," *The Times*, April 13, 1994; Paris Radio France International, April 13, 1994, 2130 GMT, in FBIS-AFR-94-072, April 14, 1994, p. 4; "Forces gouvernementales et rebelles se disputent le contrôle de la capitale," *Le Monde*, April 14, 1994; "Rwandan Rebels Prepare Last Push," *The Times*, April 14, 1994).

9. Keith Richburg, "Rwanda Rebels Call Truce, but Bloodshed Goes On," *Washington Post*, April 27, 1994; Patrick Mazimhaka, interview with author, Kigali, April 23, 1999.

10. "Strife in Rwanda: The Fighting," *New York Times*, April 11, 1994, p. A-12; "Le Rwanda à feu et à sang"; "Forces gouvernementales et rebelles"; Jean Hélène, "Les combats continuent au Rwanda," *Le Monde*, April 15, 1994, p. 1; Paris Radio France International, 1830 GMT, April 15, 1994, in FBIS-AFR-94-074, p. 2; London BBC World Service, 1705 GMT, April 17, 1994, in FBIS-AFR-94-074, April 18, 1994, p. 4.

11. Brussels La Une Radio Network, 1500 GMT, April 18, 1994, in FBIS-WEU-94-075, April 19, 1994, p. 5.

12. (Clandestine) Radio Muhabura, 1100 GMT, April 13, 1994, in FBIS-AFR-94-072, April 14, 1994, p. 2.

13. "Convention on the Prevention and Punishment of the Crime of Genocide," UN General Assembly, adopted December 9, 1948.

14. Press Release, Human Rights Watch/Africa, April 20, 1994. The HRW estimate was also contained in a private letter to the president of the UN Security Council on the previous day, April 19, 1994; the ICRC estimate is cited in Drumtra, "Rwanda: Genocide," p. 4.

15. For example, Ben Barber ("Kosovo, E. Timor Casualties Inflated," *Washington Times*, November 9, 1999, p. 1), reported that on-site investigation after reported atrocities in Kosovo and East Timor led to "cuts in the estimated death toll" by a factor of ten or more. Likewise, George Kenney ("The Bosnia Calculation: How Many Have Died?" *New York Times Magazine*, April 23, 1995), has asserted that death estimates during the war in Bosnia were inflated three to eight times.

16. *Lettre ouverte aux parlementaires: Le texte du rapport du groupe "Rwanda" du Senat* (Brussels: Editions Luc Pire, 1997), p. 129.

17. Alison Des Forges, e-mail communications to author, December 21, 1997, and January 22, 1998.

18. Paris Europe No. 1 Radio, 0540 GMT, April 11, 1994, in FBIS-WEU-94-070, April 12, 1994; Brussels La Une Radio Network, 1600 GMT, April 11, 1994, in FBIS-AFR-940-070, April 12, 1994; Spanish report cited in "Rebels Advance in Rwanda, Vow to Take Over Capital," *Washington Post*, April 12, 1994.

19. BBC World Service, 1515 GMT, April 12, 1994, in FBIS-AFR-94-071, April 13, 1994, p. 4 (emphasis added); (Clandestine) Radio Muhabura, 1645 GMT, April 13, 1994, in FBIS-AFR-94-072, April 14, 1994, p. 5; (Clandestine) Radio Muhabura, 1045 GMT, April 14, 1994, in FBIS-AFR-94-073, April 15, 1994, p. 2.

20. "Embattled UN Clings to Hope of Rwanda Truce," *The Times*, April 16, 1994, p. 14, and in American newspapers. It appears this story was reported the previous day on Belgian radio, which however located the massacre "not far from Kigali" (Radio Vlaanderen, 0900 GMT, April 15, 1994, in FBIS-AFR-94-073, April 15, 1994, p. 3). (Clandestine) Radio Muhabura, 1815 GMT, April 16, 1994; and BBC World Service, 1705 GMT, April 16, 1994, both in FBIS-AFR-94-074, p. 6, April 18, 1994. "Les <<casques bleus>> belges s'apprêtent à quitter Kigali, malgré la poursuite des combats," *Le Monde*, April 17, 1994, p. 6, citing an *El Pais* (Spain) report based on interviews with Italian soldiers evacuating foreigners in Rwanda. The massacre was reported to have occurred on April 13, 1994 (Agence France Presse, 1746 GMT, April 19, 1994, in FBIS-AFR-94-076, April 20, 1994, p. 4, citing a journalist from a Ugandan-government newspaper). Most of these massacres were on the path of the RPA's eastern offensive.

21. (Clandestine) Radio Muhabura, 1815 GMT, April 19, 1994, in FBIS-AFR-94-076, April 20, 1994, p. 4; *Fact Sheet on Rwanda*, U.S. Committee for Refugees, April 19, 1994; Brussels Radio Vlaanderen, 0900 GMT, April 21, 1994, in FBIS-AFR-94-077, April 21, 1994; Brussels La Une Radio Network, 1100 GMT, April 21, 1994, in FBIS-AFR-94-078, April 22, 1994.

22. "Special Report of the Secretary-General on UNAMIR, Containing a Summary of the Developing Crisis in Rwanda and Proposing Three Options for the Role of the United Nations in Rwanda," S/1994/47, April 20, 1994, in *The United Nations and Rwanda: 1993–1996* (New York: United Nations, Department of Public Information, 1996), p. 262.

23. "Westerners Begin Fleeing Rwanda," *Washington Post*, April 10, 1994, p. A1.

24. (Clandestine) Radio Muhabura, 1900 GMT, April 17, 1994, in FBIS-AFR-94-075, April 19, 1994.

25. For example, in the Democratic Republic of Congo, false claims of anti-Tutsi genocide were made in 1998; see *UN Integrated Regional Information Network for Central and Eastern Africa*, Update No. 490, August 28, 1998.

26. Letter from Human Rights Watch to UN Security Council, April 19, 1994;

Drumtra, "Rwanda: Genocide," p. 4. Alison Des Forges claims she discussed the substance of the Human Rights Watch letter with international diplomats several days before sending it on April 19. She says that on April 21 she spoke to Madeleine Albright, then U.S. ambassador to the United Nations, who indicated she already knew genocide was under way (Des Forges, e-mail communication to author, January 22, 1998). See also Des Forges, *Leave None*, pp. 286, 642.

27. Former senior DIA Africa analyst, interviews with author, February 16, 18, and 25, 2001.

28. Ibid.

29. Official at the State Department's Bureau of Intelligence and Research who worked on Rwanda during the genocide, interview with author, February 20, 2001.

30. Former officials of the State Department, National Security Council, and Pentagon who worked on Rwanda during the genocide, interviews with author.

31. State Department official, interview with author, January 19, 2001. The task force comprised approximately three dozen officials who worked in three eight-hour shifts.

32. Former senior DIA Africa analyst, interviews with author, February 16, 18, and 25, 2001. Official at the State Department's Bureau of Intelligence and Research who worked on Rwanda during the genocide, interview with author, February 20, 2001.

33. Former Pentagon director for Africa (in the office of the assistant secretary for international security affairs), interview with author, February 20, 2001. Former senior DIA Africa analyst, interviews with author, February 16, 18, and 25, 2001.

34. Former NSC official, interviews with author, January 23, 2001, and February 20, 2001. Former senior DIA Africa analyst, interviews with author, February 16, 18, and 25, 2001.

35. Former NSC official, interviews with author, January 23, 2001, and February 20, 2001.

36. This is the belief of the former senior DIA Africa analyst, interviews with author, February 16, 18, and 25, 2001.

37. Former senior DIA Africa analyst, interviews with author, February 16, 18, and 25, 2001.

38. Former NSC official, interview with author, February 20, 2001.

39. Former senior NSC official, interviews with author, January 23, 2001, and February 20, 2001.

40. Official at the State Department's Bureau of Intelligence and Research who worked on Rwanda during the genocide, interview with author, February 20, 2001.

41. Former Pentagon director for Africa (in the office of the assistant secretary for international security affairs), interview with author, February 20, 2001.

42. Daniel Patrick Moynihan, "What We Knew and Why We Didn't Know Sooner," *Washington Post*, March 17, 2001, p. A21.

Chapter Five

1. Estimates of the FAR's size in 1994 vary. For example, according to Gérard Prunier it was "close to 50,000"; Filip Reyntjens: 30,000 to 40,000; General Dallaire: 28,000 to 30,000; UNAMIR's deputy commander General Henry Anyidoho: 36,000, including the gendarmerie; see Commission d'enquête parlementaire concernant les événements du Rwanda, *Rapport* (Brussels: Senat de Belgique, December 6, 1997), hereafter cited as *Belgian Senate Report*, testimony of René Lemarchand, section 3.6.4.1.; testimony of Gérard Prunier, section 3.6.4.2; and section 3.3.3.11; Bernard Lugan, *Histoire du Rwanda* (Etrepilly, France: Bartillat, 1997), p. 502; Henry Kwami Anyidoho, *Guns over Kigali* (Accra, Ghana: Woeli Publishing Services, 1997), pp. 111–13; Scott R. Feil, *Preventing Genocide: How the Early Use of Force Might Have Succeeded in Rwanda* (New York: Carnegie Corporation of New York, 1998), p. 37.

2. *Belgian Senate Report*, section 3.6.4.2; Lugan, *Histoire du Rwanda*, p. 502. See also Feil, *Preventing Genocide*, p. 38; Alison Des Forges, *Leave None to Tell the Story: Genocide in Rwanda* (New York: Human Rights Watch, 1999), pp. 55, 227–31; Ntaribi Kamanzi, *Rwanda: Du Génocide a la Défaite* (Kigali: Editions Rebero, 1997), pp. 41, 48. For a summary of the self-defense force, see Des Forges, *Leave None*, p. 278.

3. Anyidoho, *Guns over Kigali*, pp. 111–13.

4. Adding some confusion, two different versions of the rules were circulated; see Des Forges, *Leave None*, pp. 133–34, 596–97.

5. True to its name, the UN Observation Mission Uganda-Rwanda (UNOMUR) observed, but rarely if ever stopped, arms transfers between Uganda and northern Rwanda; see, for example, Gérard Prunier, *The Rwanda Crisis: History of a Genocide* (New York: Columbia University Press, 1995), p. 194, n. 3.

6. Alison Des Forges, e-mail communication to author, January 8, 1998.

7. See, for example, R. M. Connaughton, *Military Support and Protection for Humanitarian Assistance: Rwanda, April–December 1994* (Camberley: England: Strategic and Combat Studies Institute, 1995), pp. 25–26; Prunier, *The Rwanda Crisis*, pp. 234–37; Larry Minear and Philippe Guillot, *Soldiers to the Rescue: Humanitarian Lessons from Rwanda* (Paris: Development Centre of the OECD, 1996), p. 95. Anyidoho (*Guns over Kigali*, pp. 33, 50–51) discloses that UNAMIR violated the troop cap of 270. Some 356 Ghanaians constituted the bulk of the remaining troops.

8. UNAMIR's deputy commander estimates the RPF's prewar strength as 20,000. Prunier estimates their strength on April 6 as 20,000–25,000 and explains that it grew as the RPF captured Rwanda during the genocide and Tutsi refugees flocked to join its cause. Lower estimates of 13,000 and 17,000 are quoted by Minear and Guillot. The Carnegie Commission estimates 12,000. See Anyidoho, *Guns over Kigali*, p. 113; Prunier, *The Rwanda Crisis*, p. 270; Minear and Guillot, *Soldiers to the Rescue*, pp. 60–63; Feil, *Preventing Genocide*, p. 37.

9. RPF officials, interviews with author, Kigali, April 1999; Kamanzi, *Rwanda*; Anyidoho, *Guns over Kigali*, pp. 30–32; African Rights, *Rwanda: Death, Despair*, pp. 1062–84; Lugan, *Histoire du Rwanda*, pp. 506–7.

10. Anyidoho, *Guns over Kigali*, p. 114.

11. For background on the genesis of the operation in France, see Prunier, *The Rwanda Crisis*, pp. 281–99.

12. Graham T. Allison, *Essence of Decision: Explaining the Cuban Missile Crisis* (Boston: Little, Brown, 1971), p. 6; Morton Halperin, *Bureaucratic Politics and Foreign Policy* (Brookings Institution, 1974).

13. Des Forges, *Leave None*, pp. 655–57, 661–66; Kamanzi, *Rwanda*, pp. 182–90; Prunier, *The Rwanda Crisis*, pp. 281–99.

14. Des Forges, *Leave None*, pp. 655–57, 661–66.

15. J. Matthew Vaccaro, "The Politics of Genocide: Peacekeeping and Rwanda," in William Durch, ed., *UN Peacekeeping, American Politics, and the Uncivil Wars of the 1990s* (New York: St. Martin's, 1996), p. 385; Amiral Jacques Lanxade, "L'opération Turquoise," *Défense Nationale* (February 1995), pp. 7–16; *French Parliamentary Report on Military Operations in Rwanda between 1990 and 1994*, no. 1271, section VII.C.1 (www.assemblee-nat.fr/2/dossiersrwanda/r1271.htm) (hereafter *French Parliamentary Report*); Lugan, *Histoire du Rwanda*, p. 510.

16. Lanxade, "L'opération Turquoise."

17. Ibid. A previous study by Minear and Guillot reports erroneously that the entire 8,100 metric tons was airlifted to the theater during the first week (see Minear and Guillot, *Soldiers to the Rescue*, p. 95). This would have been physically impossible given the constraints at Goma and the limited number of airlifters, and the estimate is probably too high by a factor of five. The nominal payloads of the Il-76 and An-124 are 40 and 150 metric tons, respectively. However, their realistic payloads on long routes are probably considerably smaller. Russian aircraft have better maneuverability than U.S. aircraft on runways, but the Goma airfield during Turquoise still never held more than four large strategic lifters at one time. Goma was aided somewhat by a portable radar system. The fuel demanded by the operation threatened to shut down commercial aviation in Central Africa; see David C. Isby, *Weapons and Tactics of the Soviet Army*, new ed. (London: Jane's, 1988), p. 401; senior official, Directorate of Strategic Affairs, French Ministry of Defense, interview with author, Paris, June 6, 1997.

18. Senior official, Directorate of Strategic Affairs, French Ministry of Defense, interview with author, Paris, June 6, 1997; Lanxade, "L'opération Turquoise"; Des Forges, *Leave None*, pp. 668–76, 684. See also the following reports by Raymond Bonner in the *New York Times*: "Rwandan Enemies Struggle to Define French Role," June 27, 1994; "French in Rwanda Discover Thousands of Hutu Refugees," June 28, 1994; "Fear Is Still Pervasive in Rwanda Countryside," June 29, 1994; "Tutsi Refugees Reported Trapped in Rwanda," June 30, 1994; "Grisly Discovery in Rwanda Leads French to Widen Role," July 1, 1994; "As French Aid the Tutsi, Backlash Grows," July 2, 1994; "French Force in Skirmish in Rwanda," July 4, 1994; "French Establish a Base in

Rwanda to Block Rebels," July 5, 1994; "France Backs Away from Battle in Rwanda," July 6, 1994.

19. Lanxade, "L'opération Turquoise"; Des Forges, *Leave None*, pp. 668–76, 684.

20. Events leading to the initial firefight are described in "After Genocide: A Conversation with Paul Kagame," *Transition*, no. 72 (1996), pp. 171–74. The rebels raced toward Butare seeking a confrontation with a French unit there, but by the time they arrived the unit had moved on to Gikongoro. The French unit then asked the RPF for permission to return to Butare to retrieve some Rwandans. General Paul Kagame granted permission but then ambushed the French troops on their return to Gikongoro and insisted on inspecting the French vehicles. The confrontation was relatively peaceful until rebels found several FAR troops hidden in the French vehicles and shot them when they tried to escape. Some French troops thought the rebels were firing on them and a brief firefight ensued.

21. The forces at Kibuye and Gikongoro were French marines, led respectively by Colonels Patrice Sartre and Jacques Rosier. Those at Cyangugu were legion troops led by Lt. Col. Jacques Hogard (who apparently used various aliases, judging from reports of a commander at Cyangugu named Colonel "Thibault," "Thibaut," or "Tauzin.") The entire operation was led by General Jean Claude Lafourcade; see Yves DeBay, *Troupes de Marine* (Paris: Histoire & Collection, 1996), pp. 54, 76; Vaccaro, "The Politics of Genocide," pp. 387–88; Anyidoho, *Guns over Kigali*, p. 102; Des Forges, *Leave None*, pp. 674–75; *French Parliamentary Report*, section VII.C.1.

22. Des Forges, *Leave None*, p. 684; Kamanzi, *Rwanda*, pp. 187, 190.

23. Senior official, Directorate of Strategic Affairs, French Ministry of Defense, interview with author, Paris, June 6, 1997.

24. DeBay, *Troupes de Marine*, pp. 54, 76; "After Genocide: A Conversation with Paul Kagame," pp. 171–74.

25. Prunier cites two different population figures: 1.2 million and 1.5 million (*The Rwanda Crisis*, pp. 299, 311).

26. Senior official, Directorate of Strategic Affairs, French Ministry of Defense, interview with author, Paris, June 6, 1997; articles by Bonner in the *New York Times* on July 1 and July 2, 1994 (see note 7); Des Forges, *Leave None*, pp. 679–82.

27. African Rights, *Rwanda: Death, Despair*, p. 1147–49; Prunier, *The Rwanda Crisis*, p. 293. See also Victoria Brittain, "French Abandoned Wounded Tutsis; Genocide Survivors Left to Face Killers, Report Says," *Guardian*, April 3, 1998; Bonner article in the *New York Times* on June 28, 1994 (see note 7).

28. Vaccaro, "The Politics of Genocide," p. 387; Lanxade, "L'opération Turquoise," pp. 12–13.

29. Anyidoho, *Guns over Kigali*, pp. 102, 105; Lanxade, "L'opération Turquoise," pp. 11–13.

30. African Rights, *Rwanda: Death, Despair*, p. 1150; Des Forges, *Leave None*, p. 685, 689.

31. See "Report of the International Commission of Inquiry on the Flow of Arms to Former Rwandan Forces," United Nations, November 23, 1998.

Chapter Six

1. Alain Rouvez, with the assistance of Michael Coco and Jean-Paul Paddack, *Disconsolate Empires: French, British, and Belgian Military Involvement in Post-Colonial Sub-Saharan Africa* (Lanham, Md.: University Press of America, 1994), pp. 331–40; Peter Mangold, "Shaba I and Shaba II," *Survival*, vol. 21 (May/June 1979), p. 111; Lt. Col. Thomas P. Odom, *Shaba II: The French and Belgian Intervention in Zaire in 1978* (Fort Leavenworth: U.S. Army Command and General Staff College, 1993).

2. Rouvez, *Disconsolate Empires*, p. 340.

3. Colonel Spartacus, *Operation Manta: Les Documents Secrets* (Paris: Librairie Plon, 1985), pp. 50–58, 245–53; Rouvez, *Disconsolate Empires*, pp. 155–59; Keith Somerville, *Foreign Military Intervention in Africa* (New York: St. Martin's, 1990), pp. 70–71.

4. John Lund, Ruth Berg, and Corinne Replogle, *An Assessment of Strategic Airlift Efficiency*, R-4269/4-AF (Santa Monica, Calif.: Rand, 1993), pp. 36–38.

5. James A. Winnefeld, Preston Niblack, and Dana J. Johnson, *A League of Airmen: U.S. Air Power in the Gulf War* (Santa Monica, Calif.: Rand, 1994), p. 31.

6. The nominal capacity included 37.2 MTM/D of dedicated airlift and 11.3 MTM/D of the civil reserve air fleet (CRAF). Thus even if the nominal reserve air fleet capacity were excluded, the actual first month lift of eleven MTM/D represented only 30 percent of nominal dedicated lift capacity. See Douglas Menarchik, *Powerlift—Getting to Desert Storm* (Westport, Conn.: Praeger, 1993), p. 34, n. 41; Congressional Budget Office, *Moving U.S. Forces: Options for Strategic Mobility* (Washington,: U.S. Government Printing Office, February 1997), p. 12.

7. Lund, Berg, and Replogle, *An Assessment*, pp. 59, 74–76, 92, 96.

8. Tom Breen and Vago Muradian, "A Journey to Hell: The Air Force Is on the Move Again," *Air Force Times*, August 8, 1994, pp. 12–13. See also Lieutenant General Daniel Schroeder, "Lessons of Rwanda," *Armed Forces Journal International*, December 1994, pp. 31–32.

9. Lieutenant General Daniel R. Schroeder, *Operation Support Hope 1994, After Action Report* (Headquarters, U.S. European Command, 1994), Appendix 2-5, 2-6, hereafter cited as *AAR*.

10. For example, a C-5 carrying a water purification system made the trip nonstop in twenty-two hours on July 25, 1994, with three aerial refuelings. See Andrew Compart, "Airmen Embark on a Mission of Mercy: Reserve and Guard Units 'Want to Help Any Way They Can,'" *Air Force Times*, August 8, 1994, p. 14.

11. Schroeder, *AAR*, pp. 14–18, appendix slide data.

12. Ibid., pp. 12, 15, Appendix 2-7. The Joint Task Force formally designated four bases as Rear (Stuttgart), Main (Entebbe), Forward (Kigali), and Tactical (Goma). Nairobi also served as an overnight rest stop for flight crews.

13. Lieutenant General Daniel Schroeder, USA (Ret.), interview with author, February 8, 1999; Breen and Muradian, "A Journey to Hell." Shell was already the primary fuel contractor in the region. Each Air Force team is known as a Tanker/Air-

Lift Control Element (TALCE). They were deployed to Mildenhall (United Kingdom), Moron (Spain), Souda Bay (Crete), Addis Ababa, Entebbe, Goma, Kigali, Mombasa, Harare, and Nairobi. In Nairobi the deployment was officially designated a Mission Support Team (MST), rather than a TALCE, because it was managed by an enlisted member.

14. Lund, Berg, and Replogle, *An Assessment,* pp. 58–61, 96.

15. Lieutenant General Edward M. Flanagan, Jr., USA (Ret.), *Lightning: The 101st in the Gulf War* (Washington: Brassey's, 1994), pp. 39, 50, 54–55. Load-out of the 101st ready brigade was conducted during approximately August 16–29, 1990. Flanagan reports that "a total of 60 C-141s and 50 C-5As carried" the task force, but this probably refers to the number of sorties rather than aircraft. For citations on load-out of the 82d ready brigade, see Appendix C.

16. Lund, Berg, and Replogle, *An Assessment.*

17. Schroeder, *AAR,* Appendix 2-5. Schroeder, in an interview with author, February 8, 1999, explained that each instance of airborne refueling occupies the air space for a protracted period.

18. Lund, Berg, and Replogle, *An Assessment,* pp. 58–61, 96.

19. Schroeder, *AAR,* Appendix 2-6.

20. Ibid., Appendix 2-7. Schroeder, interview with author, February 8, 1999. At nominal maximum payloads, never attained in practice, the maximum throughput was 567 tons.

21. James P. Stucker and Ruth T. Berg, *Understanding Airfield Capacity for Airlift Operations* (Santa Monica, Calif.: Rand, 1998), p. xi.

22. Henry Kwami Anyidoho, *Guns over Kigali* (Accra, Ghana: Woeli Publishing Services, 1997), pp. 75–77.

23. Schroeder, *AAR,* Appendix 2-6. TACC is based at Scott Air Force Base in Illinois.

24. Ibid. These quoted statistics appear to be based on canonical estimates rather than empirical evidence.

25. Throughput = (maximum on ground) x (payload) x (operating hours/turnaround time). Thus, if payload and turnaround performance were 20 percent worse than expectations, capacity would be 1,512 x .8 / 1.2 ~ 1,000 tons. If payload were 20 percent worse than expectations, but turnaround time 50 percent worse, capacity would be 1,512 x .8 / 2 ~ 600 tons. In Operation Desert Shield, the Dhahran airfield was so crowded that "sometimes refueling took 6 to 7 hours," more than double the canonical two to three hours. During the first month of the operation, the average ground time at theater airfields was 20–30 percent longer than planned. See Menarchik, *Powerlift,* pp. 74, 81–82.

26. This maximum rate would require eighteen C-5 and thirty-six C-141 sorties per day, based on the payloads of Desert Shield ([18 C-5 x 60 tons] + [36 C-141 x 20 tons] = 1,800 tons). Assuming a four-day round trip and a 67 percent aircraft availability rate, the job would have required 108 C-5 aircraft (18 C-5 x 4-day round trip / 0.67 availability = 108 C-5 aircraft) and, by similar calculation, 216 C-141 aircraft. As

noted in the text, the total U.S. fleet of these aircraft employed during Operation Desert Shield in 1991 was 110 C-5 and 234 C-141 aircraft. The fleet had not changed considerably by 1994.

27. Schroeder, *AAR*, Appendix 2-6.

28. Self-deployment of helicopters would have yielded only a modest airlift reduction, because their associated maintenance and force-protection equipment and personnel would have had to be airlifted before the helicopters could be deployed into the field. See, for example, the experience of Task Force Hawk in Kosovo in 1999.

29. Michael O'Hanlon, *Saving Lives with Force: Military Criteria for Humanitarian Intervention* (Brookings Institution, 1997).

Chapter Seven

1. See James T. Quinlivan, "Force Requirements in Stability Operations," *Parameters* (Winter 1995–96), pp. 59–69.

2. Alison Des Forges, *Leave None to Tell the Story: Genocide in Rwanda* (New York: Human Rights Watch, 1999), p. 602.

3. Lt. Col. Martin N. Stanton, "Operational Considerations for Sub-Saharan Africa," *Infantry* (September–October 1996), notes that organization of such peace enforcement operations should be guided by the three types of units required: (1) "Independent combined arms maneuver columns"; (2) "Reaction force elements consisting mainly of attack helicopters and airborne or air assault infantry"; and (3) "Security elements consisting of mainly light infantry or military police for site or base security, dismounted patrolling," and related activities. In Rwanda, the first would be required for stopping the war and finding large groups of Tutsi threatened by genocide; the second for responding quickly to confrontations with armed elements; and the third for patrolling Kigali and guarding the large groups of Tutsi.

4. Newspaper reports of the period quote various pregenocide population figures for Kigali: 200,000 (Reuters, April 11, 1994); 232,000 (*Washington Post*, April 16, 1994); and 300,000 (*New York Times*, April 16, 1994). One expert stated more recently: "It is widely accepted that before the 1994 conflict, around 280,000 people lived in Kigali" (see interview with George Weber, secretary general of the International Federation of Red Cross and Red Crescent Societies, September 3, 1998, www.reliefweb.int). However, tens of thousands of capital residents would already have been dead before the United States intervened. See Quinlivan, "Force Requirements," for a discussion of force requirements in policing operations.

5. Scott R. Feil, *Preventing Genocide: How the Early Use of Force Might Have Succeeded in Rwanda* (New York: Carnegie Corporation of New York, 1998), p. 20.

6. At the time, an ACF nominally could load out in less than twenty-four hours. However, it contained only about 1,300 marines and twenty light armored vehicles and was centered on a single large infantry battalion complemented by artillery, engineer, logistics, reconnaissance, and air-defense units. Thus, to accomplish a brigade-size

mission, an ACF would have had to be reinforced with substantial quantities of infantry and transportation assets—that is, helicopters and motorized vehicles (Lieutenant Colonel John Turner, USMC, interview with author, 1997).

7. The weight of each division in tons is: air assault: 35,860; airborne: 26,699; light infantry: 17,092. The number of personnel: air assault: 15,840; airborne: 13,242; light infantry: 11,036. The number of helicopters: air assault: 380; airborne: 120; light infantry: 100. See Congressional Budget Office, *Moving U.S. Forces: Options for Strategic Mobility* (Washington: U.S. Government Printing Office, February 1997), p. 80; Frances M. Lussier, *An Analysis of U.S. Army Helicopter Programs* (Washington: Congressional Budget Office, December 1995), p. 66.

8. Stanton, "Operational Considerations," p. 31, notes: "Neither light infantry, airborne, nor air assault units have enough rolling stock to haul their organic infantry. These units will have to be augmented with either transportation units (five-ton trucks) or locally contracted vehicles. In addition their antitank companies will have to reconfigure for low intensity conflict—specifically, leaving their TOW (anti-tank weapons) systems at home station and carrying a mix of .50 caliber machineguns and Mk 19s." UNAMIR's deputy commander notes that the motorized vehicles needed were light vehicles, not armored personnel carriers, which were unsuitable for much of Rwanda's terrain; see Henry Kwami Anyidoho, *Guns over Kigali* (Accra, Ghana: Woeli Publishing Services, 1997), p. 103.

9. The paratroop operation would have been necessary unless advance permission to land had been obtained from both sides in the civil war. The rangers likely could have staged out of Entebbe, in light of Ugandan president Yoweri Museveni's antipathy for the extremist Hutu who succeeded Habyarimana and Museveni's close cooperation with the United States in subsequent humanitarian activities. Alternatively, they could have staged out of Bujumbura, considering that Burundi permitted the presence of U.S. Marines there during the evacuation mission from Rwanda and had an interest in quelling Hutu-Tutsi violence in Rwanda in order to prevent an influx of refugees and a possible contagion effect. Seizing the Kigali airfield with an advance echelon of paratroopers would have permitted subsequent troops to land rather than parachute in. The rangers conducted a similar mission in Panama at the start of the 1989 intervention.

10. Dominic J. Caraccilo, *The Ready Brigade of the 82nd Airborne in Desert Storm* (Jefferson, N.C.: McFarland, 1993), pp. 37–38; Douglas Menarchik, *Powerlift—Getting to Desert Storm* (Westport, Conn.: Praeger, 1993), p. 51.

11. Des Forges, *Leave None*, p. 22.

12. Ibid., p. 263.

13. Ibid., pp. 255–56.

14. For example, Rwandans had fled to such sites during the 1992 Bugesera massacres. Ironically, before the 1994 genocide, these types of sites had provided genuine refuge. *Lettre ouverte aux parlementaires: Le texte du rapport du groupe "Rwanda" du Senat* (Brussels: Editions Luc Pire, 1997), pp. 77, 82ff; Anyidoho, *Guns over Kigali*,

p. 19; Bernard Lugan, *Histoire du Rwanda* (Etrepilly, France: Bartillat, 1997), p. 495; Des Forges, *Leave None*, p. 90.

15. For practical purposes, the upper limit for such camps should be about 50,000 people (see Weber, www.reliefweb.int, September 3, 1998). Reconciliation efforts, which would have been difficult but essential, are beyond the scope of this book.

16. General Edward Flanagan describes the intratheater lift of aviation fuel nearly 100 miles to FOB Cobra by the 101st division in the Gulf War. He provides three different estimates of the fuel lifted in a single day by seventy-five CH-47 sorties, ranging from 75,000 to 145,000 gallons. See General Edward M. Flanagan, Jr., USA (Ret.), *Lightning: The 101st in the Gulf War* (Washington: Brassey's, 1994), pp. 167, 174.

17. Total search time = 10,000 square miles / 10 full-time helicopter units / (75 MPH x 2 miles) = 6.67 hours of searching. Over open territory in good weather the search radius would have been at least three miles. To be conservative, and to account for Rwanda's hilly terrain and heavy foliage, I assume a smaller search radius of one mile (e-mail communication to author, July 12, 1999, from Lieutenant C. D. Godinez, USN, who has flown search-and-rescue missions). Note that miles and MPH refer to ground speed, whereas air speed is measured in nautical miles and knots.

18. Professor Ted Postol, Massachusetts Institute of Technology, personal communication; Des Forges, *Leave None*, p. 219; Lussier, *An Analysis of U.S. Army Helicopter Programs*, p. xii.

19. Lieutenant General Daniel Schroeder, USA (Ret.), interview with author, February 8, 1999.

20. Interestingly, France cites the U.S. Operation Provide Comfort, which protected Kurds in northern Iraq in 1991, as a precedent for Operation Turquoise; see Amiral Jacques Lanxade, "L'opération Turquoise," *Défense Nationale* (February 1995), p. 13.

21. The six prefectures had a population of 3.8 million in 1991, which would have grown to about 4.2 million by April 1994, but 200,000 Tutsi in the zone were already dead before U.S. troops could have begun to arrive. It is possible the zone also would have contained Hutu displaced from eastern Rwanda by the RPA offensive.

22. Although Operation Turquoise employed approximately 3,000 troops, many stayed at the base in Goma, Zaire; only about 1,800 deployed in the zone, which had a population of 1.2–1.5 million, so the maximum ratio of troops per thousand of population was 1.5:1.

23. Major Sean Callahan, U.S. Army, e-mail communication to author, November 2, 1999.

24. Anyidoho, *Guns over Kigali*, p. 36. An article in the *Washington Post* quotes a Kosovo Liberation Army rebel as saying "there were too many" unintended KLA casualties from the NATO strike; see John Ward Anderson, "NATO's Most Lethal Airstrike Ended a Battle, Perhaps a War," *Washington Post*, June 26, 1999.

25. Mark A. Lorell, *Airpower in Peripheral Conflict: The French Experience in Africa*, R-3660-AF (Santa Monica, Calif.: Rand, 1989). See also Alain Rouvez, with the assistance of Michael Coco and Jean-Paul Paddack, *Disconsolate Empires: French, British,*

and Belgian Military Involvement in Post-Colonial Sub-Saharan Africa (Lanham, Md.: University Press of America, 1994).

26. Stanton, "Operational Considerations," p. 32.

27. Holly Burkhalter, "The Question of Genocide: The Clinton Administration and Rwanda," *World Policy Journal,* vol. 11 (Winter 1994), p. 6; Linda Melvern, "Genocide behind the Thin Blue Line," *Security Dialogue,* vol. 28 (September 1997), pp. 341–42; Ntaribi Kamanzi, *Rwanda: Du Génocide a la Défaite* (Kigali: Editions Rebero, 1997), pp. 150–51.

28. See Barry Shlachter, "Battles by Air // Strategies: Psychological Warfare Is Alive and Well in Yugoslavia as Commando Solo Broadcasts around Serbia and Millions of Leaflets Fly." *Orange County Register,* April 18, 1999; "USA/Yugoslavia: Psyop Airborne Broadcasts Received in Croatia," BBC Monitoring Media, April 12, 1999; Jeffrey B. Jones and Michael P. Mathews, "PSYOP and the Warfighting CINC," *Joint Forces Quarterly* (Summer 1995), p. 32; Stephen D. Brown, "PSYOP in Operation Uphold Democracy," *Military Review,* vol. 76 (September–October 1996), p. 61.

29. All figures for total miles of road are from Filip Reyntjens, "Rwanda," in *Africa South of the Sahara,* 24th ed. (London: Europa Publications, 1995), p. 754.

30. Among U.S. Army attack helicopters, the AH-1 Cobra has a maximum speed of 133 knots and a cruising range of almost 370 miles; the AH-64 Apache has a maximum speed of 155 knots and a range of 225 to 450 miles; the OH-58D Kiowa Warrior, an armed version of a scout helicopter, has a maximum speed of 120 knots and a cruising range of 215 miles. See Lussier, *An Analysis of U.S. Army Helicopter Programs,* pp. 10–12; Mark Hewish, "Apache—A True Multi-Role Helicopter," *International Defense Review,* December 1991.

Chapter Eight

1. Commission d'enquête parlementaire concernant les événements du Rwanda, *Rapport* (Brussels: Senat de Belgique, December 6, 1997) , section 3.8.4.2, author's translations (www.senate.be/docs); hereafter cited as *Belgian Senate Report.*

2. Yael Aronoff wrote in the *Washington Post* that Rwanda was never discussed at a single top-level Clinton administration meeting during the genocide because of the lack of such a policy; see Yael S. Aronoff, "Clinton's Rwanda Apology Is Fine, but America Needs to Act," *Washington Post,* April 10, 1998.

3. Holly Burkhalter, "A Preventable Horror?" *Africa Report* (November–December 1994), p. 21, which quotes a military official stating: "There was a PDD [presidential directive] on peace-keeping, and it prevented us responding on Rwanda. Unfortunately there is no PDD on genocide." Burkhalter also testified that "if it were the policy of the U.S. government to respond vigorously and affirmatively to genocide, a different outcome might be possible" (Holly Burkhalter, Physicians for Human Rights, "The 1994 Rwandan Genocide and U.S. Policy," testimony before the House Subcommittee on Human Rights and International Operations, May 5, 1998).

4. Alison Des Forges, *Leave None to Tell the Story: Genocide in Rwanda* (New York: Human Rights Watch, 1999), pp. 24–26, 641. See also a similar argument by her erstwhile Human Rights Watch colleague, Holly Burkhalter: "President Clinton ... did far too little to stigmatize and isolate the perpetrators of genocide, refusing, for example, to engage in active diplomacy to enlist Rwanda's European donors in a joint statement warning the coup participants of the consequences of genocide" (Burkhalter, "A Preventable Horror?" p. 21).

5. Des Forges, *Leave None*, pp. 194–96. Reyntjens confirms that a leading moderate army officer made such an appeal. Filip Reyntjens, Rwanda: *Trois jours qui ont fait basculer l'histoire* (Paris: Editions L'Harmattan, 1995), p. 84;

6. Alison Des Forges, e-mail communications to author, December 1997, January 1998, and August 15, 1998; fax communication to author, November 5, 1998.

7. Reyntjens, *Rwanda: Trois jours*, pp. 51–58, 86, 91, 119, author's translation. See also Des Forges, *Leave None*, pp. 194–96, 204–5, 268–69, 616. The Presidential Guard and the reconnaissance battalion, consisting of well-trained troops equipped with armored vehicles, were led respectively by Protais Mpiranya and François-Xavier Nzuwonemeye, both extremists. Reyntjens estimates their combined strength as about 1,000, Des Forges at least 1,600. The paracommando battalion, comprising Rwanda's other 500 well-trained troops, was led by Aloys Ntabuakuze, thought to have been an extremist but who may have had moderate sympathies. Other extremists with strong followings included senior officers who recently had been cashiered as part of Habyarimana's pluralization effort. At the time of the plane crash, Bagosora found a power vacuum. Defense Minister Augustin Bizimana and the G2 (intelligence) director Colonel Aloys Ntiwiragabo were in Cameroon; the G3 (military operations) director Colonel Gratien Kabiligi was in Egypt; and the army chief of staff, General Deo Nsabimana, had been killed with the president. Bagosora took de facto control by forming a crisis committee and then orchestrating the formation of a new government, which was sworn in on April 9.

8. Henry Kwami Anyidoho, *Guns over Kigali* (Accra, Ghana: Woeli Publishing Services, 1997), pp. 112–13. Admittedly, during the first days of the renewed war in Kigali, the rebels had the advantage of being on the defensive. When the rebels switched to the offensive, the army managed to hold off their complete capture of Kigali for nearly three months.

9. Leading moderate FAR officer, interview with author, Kigali, April 1999; Reyntjens, *Rwanda: Trois jours*, p. 84; Filip Reyntjens, letter to author, November 3, 1998; Des Forges, *Leave None*, pp. 194–96, 204–5, 268–69, 616; Ntaribi Kamanzi, *Rwanda: Du Génocide a la Défaite* (Kigali: Editions Rebero, 1997), pp. 67, 73.

10. Leading moderate FAR officer, interview with author, Kigali, April 1999. See also Reyntjens, *Rwanda: Trois jours*, pp. 82–86.

11. Des Forges, *Leave None*, pp. 9, 224, 263, 265, 268, 273–74, 277; Kamanzi, *Rwanda*, pp. 106–7, 126, 129.

12. Des Forges, *Leave None*, pp. 9, 224, 263, 265, 268, 273–74, 277.

13. Reyntjens, *Rwanda: Trois jours,* p. 119.

14. Des Forges, *Leave None,* pp. 194–96, 204–5, 268–69, 616; see also Kamanzi, *Rwanda,* pp. 67, 73.

15. Press release, Human Rights Watch/Africa, April 25, 1994.

16. Des Forges, *Leave None,* pp. 268–69, 641.

17. Ibid., p. 283.

18. Ibid., pp. 289, 292–97.

19. Ibid., pp. 202, 291, 298.

20. *Belgian Senate Report,* section 3.6.4.1, which cites Filip Reyntjens's testimony that the Burundian assassination and coup caused Rwanda's "moderate Hutu to believe that they could not have confidence in the RPF, and, by extension, in Tutsi themselves, entering into a genocidal logic" (author's translation). See also Des Forges, *Leave None,* p. 109.

21. Des Forges, *Leave None,* pp. 6, 197–98, 690.

22. Dallaire is quoted by Linda Melvern, "Genocide behind the Thin Blue Line," *Security Dialogue,* vol. 28 (September 1997), p. 340. Dallaire's lament also was cited in a letter from U.S. senators Paul Simon and James Jeffords to President Bill Clinton, May 13, 1994, reporting on hearings before their subcommittee (Scott R. Feil, *Preventing Genocide: How the Early Use of Force Might Have Succeeded in Rwanda* [New York: Carnegie Corporation of New York, 1998], p. 1). In 1994 Dallaire also was characterized as saying privately that with more equipment and an appropriate mandate "he could have stopped the genocide from spreading with his existing contingent" of less than 2,500 peacekeepers (Burkhalter, "A Preventable Horror?" p. 18). See also Colonel Scott R. Feil, "Could 5,000 Peacekeepers Have Saved 500,000 Rwandans? Early Intervention Reconsidered," *ISD Reports* (Georgetown University Institute for the Study of Diplomacy), vol. 3 (April 1997); "UN Blocked Canadian Plan to End Slaughter, CBC Says," CP, July 2, 1998; Holly Burkhalter, "The Question of Genocide: The Clinton Administration and Rwanda," *World Policy Journal,* vol. 11 (Winter 1994), p. 6). Des Forges, *Leave None,* p. 598.

23. Feil, *Preventing Genocide,* pp. 21–22.

24. In theory, this would have been a sufficient reinforcement because there already were 2,500 UNAMIR peacekeepers present. However, because the UN troops were generally poorly trained and poorly equipped, further reinforcements would have been necessary for an effective operation.

25. Congressional Budget Office, *Moving U.S. Forces: Options for Strategic Mobility* (Washington: U.S. Government Printing Office, February 1997), p. 80; Feil, *Preventing Genocide,* pp. 12, 16, 20.

26. Lieutenant General Daniel Schroeder, commander of Operation Support Hope, estimates: "Given the political will to do it, you could probably have had a multinational force in place within a week to 10 days." However, he gives no indication of the size and composition of this multinational force. See "UN Blocked Canadian Plan to End Slaughter."

27. Feil, *Preventing Genocide*, pp. 3, 9, 22, 26, 41. Dallaire testified in 1998, "We had a time frame of about two weeks, easily, where we could have made the task of killing much more difficult for these people"; see Stephen Buckley, "Mass Slaughter Was Avoidable, General Says," *Washington Post*, February 26, 1998.

28. Des Forges, *Leave None*, pp. 209–11, confirms this and notes that the worst massacres began April 11, 1994, only five days after Habyarimana's assassination.

29. Feil, *Preventing Genocide*, p. 52, n. 7.

30. Ibid., pp. 11, 15, 16, 18, 20.

31. Ibid., pp. 16, 18.

32. General Henry H. Shelton, "Contingency Operations in an Uncertain World: The Case of Haiti," *Strategic Review* (Fall 1998), p. 37. Ultimately, the intervention was modified two hours before the arrival of U.S. troops, when a political deal was reached; see Ann Devroy and John F. Harris, "'Leave Now,' Clinton Tells Haitian Rulers; Final Military Preparations Underway; Ultimatums to Be Delivered in Person," *Washington Post*, September 16, 1994, p. 1; and *Cosmopolitan World Atlas* (Rand McNally, 1993), p. 258. The Dominican Republic's population was about two-thirds that of Rwanda, and its area twice as big. Panama's population was less than one-third that of Rwanda, and its area three times as big (see Appendix B for sources).

33. Des Forges, *Leave None*, p. 176, citing National Security Adviser Anthony Lake. "UN Commander Interviewed on Security, Transition," BBC World Service, February 23, 1994, in FBIS-AFR-94-037.

34. Lindsey Hilsum, "UN Suppressed Warning of Rwanda Genocide Plan," *The Observer*, November 26, 1995; Charles Trueheart, "UN Inaction Cited in Rwanda Slaughter," *Washington Post*, September 25, 1997; Philip Gourevitch, "The Genocide Fax," *New Yorker*, May 11, 1998; Mike Robinson and Ben Loeterman, producers, "The Triumph of Evil," *Frontline*, PBS-TV, January 26, 1999. A copy of the cable, dated January 11, 1994, from General Dallaire in Kigali to General Baril in UN peacekeeping headquarters in New York (DPKO), is in possession of the author.

35. Belgian cables based on the same informant reported slightly different claims: 600–900 Interahamwe who could kill 1,000 victims per hour; see Reyntjens, *Rwanda: Trois jours*, p. 60.

36. *Lettre ouverte aux parlementaires: Le texte du rapport du groupe "Rwanda" du Senat* (Brussels: Editions Luc Pire, 1997), pp. 91–92.

37. To the credit of Human Rights Watch, Des Forges does quote this passage (*Leave None*, p. 151).

38. This was also the author's personal experience while serving as a fellow at the U.S. Agency for International Development, where his responsibilities included the daily review of classified cable traffic from regions of conflict.

39. Quoted by Philip Gourevitch, *We Wish to Inform You That Tomorrow We Will Be Killed with Our Families* (New York: Farrar Straus and Giroux, 1998), p. 106. Riza further stated in 1998: "We did not give that information the importance and the correct interpretation that it deserved. We realized that only in hindsight." See "UN Official Says Failed to Act on Rwanda Warning," Reuters, December 7, 1998.

40. Des Forges, *Leave None*, pp. 152–56, 174; *Lettre ouverte*, pp. 71–72, 93.

41. "Statement by the President of the Security Council," United Nations, February 17, 1994, S/PRST/1994/8.

42. See prepared testimony of Shaharyar M. Khan, United Nations, before U.S. House Subcommittee on International Operations and Human Rights, May 5, 1998, p. 2.

43. Des Forges, *Leave None*, pp. 152–56, 174; *Lettre ouverte*, pp. 91–92.

44. *Lettre ouverte*, pp. 71–72, 93; Sue Pleming, "U.N. Mandate for Rwanda under Attack," Reuters, March 13, 1994; Des Forges, *Leave None*, pp. 147,149, reports a bizarre incident in which Belgian peacekeepers successfully seized a hidden cache of arms, ammunition, and explosives on January 3, 1994—before Dallaire had even asked the UN for permission for such raids—but then returned the weapons when the FAR claimed ownership. Subsequently, the extremists hid weapons in the homes of allied FAR officers.

45. *Lettre ouverte*, pp. 87–88; UN Security Council Resolution 872, October 5, 1993. The rules for implementing the "Kigali Weapons Secure Area" were approved by the RPF and FAR on December 24, 1993.

46. *Belgian Senate Report*, section 3.3.3.11; *Lettre ouverte*, pp. 98. On January 15, 1994, the Belgian embassy in Kigali informed Brussels that raids against weapons depots were permitted "under UNAMIR's mandate, on the condition that this operation would be conducted with the Rwandan national police. This is extremely difficult because, according to the informant, the great majority of the national police is infiltrated"; see *Lettre ouverte*, pp. 90–91, author's translation.

47. *Belgian Senate Report*, section 3.2.3.4.

48. Pleming, "UN Mandate for Rwanda"; *Belgian Senate Report*, section 3.2.3.4; Des Forges, *Leave None*, pp. 161, 190.

49. *Belgian Senate Report*, section 3.3.3.7.

50. Des Forges, *Leave None*, pp. 97, 127; Kamanzi, *Rwanda*, p. 159.

51. Media propaganda in Rwanda has been catalogued by Jean-Pierre Chrétien, *Les Médias du Génocide* (Paris: Karthala, 1995); *Lettre ouverte*, p. 64; Burkhalter, "The Question of Genocide"; *Belgian Senate Report*, section 3.11.1.2, quoting Lieutenant Marc Nees, one of UNAMIR's ad hoc intelligence officers.

52. The characterization of Radio Rwanda is by Jean-Pierre Chrétien. *Belgian Senate Report*, section 3.11.1.2, author's translation; "Genocide in Rwanda," Human Rights Watch/Africa, vol. 6 (May 1994), p. 2; Kamanzi, *Rwanda*, p. 134; *Lettre ouverte*, p. 64.

53. Lieutenant Colonel Tony Marley, USA (Ret.), former political-military adviser in the U.S. State Department's Bureau of African Affairs, interview (http://www.pbs.org/wgbh/pages/frontline/shows/evil/interviews/marley.html [November 5, 2000]); *Belgian Senate Report*, section 3.11.1.2, author's translation; Kamanzi, *Rwanda*, pp. 134, 158.

54. Reyntjens, *Rwanda: Trois jours*, p. 117, author's translation; *Lettre ouverte*, p. 126; *Belgian Senate Report*, section 3.8.4.2, author's translation; Gérard Prunier, *The*

Rwanda Crisis: History of a Genocide (New York: Columbia University Press, 1995), pp. 234–35; Des Forges, *Leave None*, pp. 607, 609.

55. Slightly different troop levels are contained in Bernard Lugan, *Histoire du Rwanda* (Etrepilly, France: Bartillat, 1997), pp. 505–06, which reports that 300 French paratroopers arrived in Kigali on April 9, 600 Belgian paracommandos on April 10, and another 400 Belgian troops on April 11, for a total of 1,300 newly deployed French and Belgian paratroopers in Kigali, compared with Reyntjens's figure of 900, in addition to the UNAMIR contingent. Des Forges, *Leave None*, p. 606, reports that hundreds more U.S. Marines were positioned just off the coast of East Africa. Reyntjens also notes that Ghana had 800 troops in Rwanda under UNAMIR, of which 200 were in Kigali, and Tunisia had sixty troops in Kigali (see *Belgian Senate Report*, section 3.8.4.2; Filip Reyntjens, letter to author, November 9, 1998).

56. FAR forces in Kigali city before the renewal of civil war included the elite Presidential Guard, paracommando and reconnaissance battalions, an artillery battalion, two logistics battalions, two military-police battalions, a gendarmerie battalion, and medical and music companies. Additional units were deployed quickly to defend the capital: the Huye battalion in southern Kigali, the Rebero battalion in eastern Kigali, a third battalion in southern Kigali, elements of four battalions from the FAR's Rulindo sector, and the Nemba battalion from the FAR's Gisenyi sector. Their weapons included 120 mm mortars, 75 mm cannons, Katyusha rockets, and 37 mm heavy machine guns (see Kamanzi, *Rwanda*, pp. 118–20).

57. See *French Parliamentary Report on Military Operations in Rwanda between 1990 and 1994*, no. 1271, section V.C.1 (www.assemblee-nat.fr/2/dossiersrwanda/r1271.htm). See also Astri Suhrke, "Dilemmas of Protection: The Log of the Kigali Battalion," in Howard Adelman and Astri Suhrke, *The Path of a Genocide: The Rwanda Crisis from Uganda to Zaire* (New Brunswick: Transaction, 1999).

58. RPF officials, interviews with author, Kigali, April 1999; Des Forges, *Leave None*, pp. 180–81, 201, 608; Prunier, *The Rwanda Crisis*, pp. 234–35. The RPF stance toward intervention was highly variable in this period. On April 10 the rebels requested that Belgian troops come to the capital. On April 12, they warned the Belgians to depart within sixty hours.

59. *Belgian Senate Report*, section 3.8.4.2, author's translation.

60. Des Forges, *Leave None*, pp. 607, 611.

61. *Lettre ouverte*, p. 134; *Belgian Senate Report*, section 3.11.1.1, quoting journalist Colette Braeckman; Reyntjens, *Rwanda: Trois jours*, p. 92; Des Forges, *Leave None*, p. 23; Kamanzi, *Rwanda*, p. 182.

62. African Rights, *Rwanda: Death, Despair*, pp. 1149ff.

63. Des Forges, *Leave None*, p. 22, 608–9.

64. Ibid., pp. 234, 251.

65. An April 12 cable reported that Colonel Bagosora was probably responsible for the attack on Habyarimana's plane, which may or may not be true but indicates Bagosora had been identified as an extremist ringleader. The Belgian government

also knew who was perpetrating the violence. On April 9 its military intelligence service reported that atrocities were being committed by "the Presidential Guard, which would be regularly accompanied by the militias—probably the Interahamwe of the MRND, and the Impuzamugambi, of the CDR" (*Lettre ouverte*, pp. 129, 132). Reyntjens, *Rwanda: Trois jours*, p. 58, reports being told by a source in Rwanda during the first week that Bagosora was directing the work of both the military and the militias.

66. In Panama, U.S. forces technically did not find Noriega during their search but exhausted him so that he sought asylum from the papal nuncio four days after the start of intervention. The Panamanian president did not surrender to U.S. forces until eleven days later. See Frederick Kempe and Jose de Cordoba, "Dictator's Dodge," *Wall Street Journal*, December 26, 1989; and Frederick Kempe, "So Noriega Is Ours," *Wall Street Journal*, January 4, 1990.

67. Alan J. Kuperman, "The Rwanda Failure," *Washington Post*, op-ed, December 29, 1998.

68. See *Lettre ouverte*, pp. 90, 94–95, 98; *Belgian Senate Report*, section 3.6.5.2, author's translations; Des Forges, *Leave None*, p. 161.

69. Dallaire originally had intended to establish a helicopter quick-reaction force, but UNAMIR's troops and equipment were inadequate; see *Belgian Senate Report*, section 3.2.3.4.

70. *Lettre ouverte*, pp. 85–86.

71. *Belgian Senate Report*, section 3.3.3.12, citing testimony of Lode Willems, chief of staff at Belgium's Foreign Affairs Ministry.

72. *Belgian Senate Report*, section 3.3.3.12, citing testimony of Lieutenant Nees. As further evidence of the extremists' willingness to challenge peacekeepers with force, on the first day of genocide FAR soldiers opened fire on Belgian troops who were guarding Rwanda's moderate opposition prime minister, disabling two of their four jeeps; see Des Forges, *Leave None*, p. 188.

73. The extremists would have known of the UN decision as soon as it was made, because Rwanda occupied one of the rotating seats on the council at the time. Interestingly, the related danger of preventive attack by extremists against peacekeepers already in Rwanda if the UN voted to increase UNAMIR's mandate and size was cited by the United States and United Kingdom in opposing such reinforcement *after* the outbreak of genocide. Des Forges, *Leave None*, p. 603.

Chapter Nine

1. *Lettre ouverte aux parlementaires: Le texte du rapport du groupe "Rwanda" du Senat* (Brussels: Editions Luc Pire, 1997), p. 134; Commission d'enquête parlementaire concernant les événements du Rwanda, *Rapport* (Brussels: Senat de Belgique, December 6, 1997) (www.senate.be/docs), section 3.6.4.5, quoting Astri Suhrke (hereafter cited as *Belgian Senate Report*).

2. *Belgian Senate Report*, section 3.3.3.11; Alison Des Forges, e-mail communication to author, January 22, 1998.

3. Battalion-level intelligence was reported by Lieutenant Nees to Major Podevijn to Belgium's defense intelligence agency. Lieutenant Nees eventually was replaced by Captain De Cuyper. Force-level intelligence was reported by Captain Claeys to Major Maggen and then to Dallaire, who conveyed it to the secretary general's special representative in Rwanda, Jacques-Roger Booh-Booh, who finally forwarded it to UN headquarters in New York. The force-level intelligence cell was the initiative of Claeys, who also made first contact with the informant, "Jean-Pierre," whose accusations were reported in the "genocide fax."

4. This information is drawn from *Belgian Senate Report*, section 3.3.3.11.

5. Alison Des Forges, *Leave None to Tell the Story: Genocide in Rwanda* (New York: Human Rights Watch, 1999), p. 142.

6. The agency's intelligence reports are rated from A1 to F6, where the letter and number indicate the reliability of the source and its information, respectively. All of the reports discussed in this book, except the one noted in the text, were rated A1 to B2. *Lettre ouverte*, p. 27.

7. *Belgian Senate Report*, section 3.3.3.11.

8. Lists containing 331 and 1,500 names were discovered in March 1993 and February 1994, respectively; see Filip Reyntjens, *Rwanda: Trois jours qui ont fait basculer l'histoire* (Paris: Editions L'Harmattan, 1995), pp. 60–61. Many other early warning signs are documented in Howard Adelman and Astri Suhrke, "Early Warning and Conflict Management," Study 2 of *The International Response to Conflict and Genocide: Lessons from the Rwanda Experience* (Copenhagen: Steering Committee of the Joint Evaluation of Emergency Assistance to Rwanda, March 1996), hereafter cited as *JEEAR*. See also *Belgian Senate Report*, section 3.5.4.5; Des Forges, *Leave None*, pp. 141ff.

9. *Lettre ouverte*, pp. 66, 69, 72, 79, 80; Reyntjens, *Rwanda: Trois jours*, p. 58; *Belgian Senate Report*, section 3.6.5.2.

10. See, for example, Philip Gourevitch, "The Genocide Fax," *New Yorker*, May 11, 1998. See also statements by Philip Gourevitch in Mike Robinson and Ben Loeterman, producers, "The Triumph of Evil," *Frontline*, PBS-TV, January 26, 1999.

11. Cited in *Lettre ouverte*, p. 84; and *JEEAR*. Alison Des Forges, in an e-mail communication to this author, January 8, 1998, and a fax to this author, November 5, 1998, confirmed that she is the original source of this claim.

12. *Belgian Senate Report*, section 3.11.1.2.

13. *Lettre ouverte*, pp. 73–75, 81–84; *Belgian Senate Report*, section 3.3.3.11; Des Forges, *Leave None*, p. 172, 622. Des Forges reports that on March 2, 1994, an informant from Habyarimana's MRND Party reportedly told Belgian officials of a plan to exterminate all Tutsi in Kigali if the RPF resumed the civil war (p. 168). However, the information may have been judged of low reliability because this cable was not included in a retrospective Belgian analysis of all intelligence rated highly reliable before the genocide.

14. *Belgian Senate Report*, section 3.3.3.11.

15. Ibid., section 3.6.5.2; Scott R. Feil, *Preventing Genocide: How the Early Use of Force Might Have Succeeded in Rwanda* (New York: Carnegie Corporation of New York, 1998), p. 6.

16. The December 3 letter is quoted in Des Forges, *Leave None*, p. 145; the Belgian cable is quoted in *Lettre ouverte*, pp. 68, 72, 81, author's translation.

17. Henry Kwami Anyidoho, *Guns over Kigali* (Accra, Ghana: Woeli Publishing Services, 1997), pp. 17–18.

18. Prunier is quoted in *Belgian Senate Report*, section 3.6.5.2, author's translation. One prediction that did come true, in late February 1994, was the attempted assassination of the moderate leaders of the Parti Social Démocrate (PSD) and the Mouvement Démocratique Républicain (MDR), which was foreseen in the December 3, 1993, anonymous letter from FAR moderates. The PSD leader, Felicien Gatabazi, was killed, and the MDR leader, Faustin Twagiramungu, escaped; see Des Forges, *Leave None*, p. 163.

19. Tony Marley, interview (www.pbs.org/wgbh/pages/frontline/shows/evil/interviews/marley.html [November 5, 2000]).

20. *Belgian Senate Report*, section 3.3.3.11.

21. *Lettre ouverte*, p. 83.

22. Ibid., pp. 68–69. The cables cite as the real villain M. Mugenzi, president of the Parti Libéral (PL), who was an RPF ally and who "rejected all compromises" proposed by Habyarimana.

23. *Belgian Senate Report*, section 3.6.5.2, author's translation.

24. Steven Edwards, "'Explosive' Leak on Rwanda Genocide: Informants Told UN Investigators They Were on Squad That Killed Rwanda's President—and a Foreign Government Helped," *National Post*, March 1, 2000. See also, "Rwanda: Judge May Issue Warrant for Kagame's Arrest," *Integrated Regional Information Networks*, October 13, 2000 (www.reliefweb.int/IRIN/cea/countrystories/rwanda/20001013b.phtml [November 5, 2000]). See also English translation of testimony by Jean-Pierre Mugabe, April 21, 2000 (www.multimania.com/obsac/OBSV3N16-PlaneCrash94.html [November 5, 2000]).

25. *Belgian Senate Report*, sections 3.6.5.2, 3.3.3.11, 3.8.4.2, 3.6.4.5, author's translations.

26. Des Forges, *Leave None*, p. 603; *Belgian Senate Report*, sections 3.6.5.2, 3.3.3.11, 3.8.4.2, 3.6.4.5.

27. U.S. officials handling Rwanda in April 1994 at the State Department, Pentagon, and National Security Council, interviews with author, January and February 2001.

28. Des Forges, *Leave None*, pp. 19, 623, 640; Alison Des Forges, "The Method in Rwanda's Madness; Politics, Not Tribalism, Is the Root of the Bloodletting," *Washington Post*, April 17, 1994.

29. Des Forges, *Leave None*, pp. 628, 640. For the classic discussion of this problem, see Robert Jervis, *Perception and Misperception in International Politics* (Princeton, N.J.: Princeton University Press, 1976).

Chapter Ten

1. See Alan J. Kuperman, "The Other Lesson of Rwanda: Mediators Sometimes Do More Damage Than Good," *SAIS Review*, vol. 16 (Winter–Spring 1996): 221–40.

2. Barbara F. Walter, "The Critical Barrier to Civil War Settlement," *International Organization*, vol. 51 (Summer 1997): 335–64. See also Barbara F. Walter, "Designing Transitions from Civil War: Demobilization, Democratization, and Commitments to Peace," *International Security*, vol. 24 (Summer 1999): 125–55.

3. See Alan J. Kuperman, "False Hope Abroad: Promises to Intervene Often Bring Bloodshed," *Washington Post*, June 14, 1998, Outlook Section, p. 1; Alan J. Kuperman, "Once Again, Peacekeepers Arrive Too Late," *Wall Street Journal*, op-ed, September 21, 1999; Kuperman, "The Other Lesson of Rwanda."

4. It appears that the U.S. Marines are at least beginning to take steps to coordinate their intelligence on the infrastructure of likely trouble spots. See Vernon Loeb, "A Higher IQ before the Marines Land," *Washington Post*, November 17, 2000.

5. Official at the State Department's Bureau of Intelligence and Research who worked on Rwanda during the genocide, interview with author, February 20, 2001.

6. Jonathan Steele, "Serb Killings Exaggerated by West: Claims of up to 100,000 Ethnic Albanians Massacred in Kosovo Revised to under 3,000 as Exhumations Near End," *Guardian*, August 18, 2000; Seth Mydans, "East Timor, Stuck at 'Ground Zero,' Lacks Law, Order and Much More," *New York Times*, February 16, 2000.

7. By relying on twenty-ton light armored vehicles rather than seventy-ton tanks, the new units would be lighter than existing U.S. armored brigades, but probably still heavier than the existing airborne brigades that were envisioned as the core of the intervention forces analyzed in Chapter 7. See Tom Bowman, "Army Retools to Lean Force; but Policy Is Debated as Urban Warriors Replace Heavy Armor," *Baltimore Sun*, September 4, 2000.

8. "The African Crisis Response Initiative," Summary Paper, U.S. Department of State, December 2000. The initial brigade-level training exercise took place in Senegal in September 2000. As of the end of 2000, the initiative had provided training to about 6,000 African troops from eight countries.

9. "Report of the Panel on United Nations Peace Operations," United Nations report A/55/305, S/2000/809, August 17, 2000.

10. See Alan J. Kuperman, "Transnational Causes of Genocide, or How the West Inadvertently Exacerbates Ethnic Conflict in the Post–Cold War Era," presented at the annual meeting of the American Political Science Association, Atlanta, Ga., September 2–5, 1999.

11. Lewis MacKenzie, *Peacekeeper: The Road to Sarajevo* (Vancouver, B.C.: Douglas & McIntyre, 1993); Sir Michael Rose, *Fighting for Peace: Bosnia 1994* (London: Harvill Press, 1998), p. 141. Rose reports that the Bosnian government's Muslim-led forces continued this strategy through 1994 based on the logic that "if the Bosnian Army attacked and lost, the resulting images of war and suffering guaranteed support in the West for the 'victim State.'"

Appendix A

1. Scott Feil suggests that a half-million Rwandans from Byumba and Ruhengeri prefectures remained displaced from their homes when the genocide began. See Scott R. Feil, *Preventing Genocide: How the Early Use of Force Might Have Succeeded in Rwanda* (New York: Carnegie Corporation of New York, 1998), p. 41.

2. Senior official, Directorate of Strategic Affairs, French Ministry of Defense, interview with author, Paris, June 6, 1997.

Appendix B

1. Colonel Albert P. Sights Jr., "Lessons of Lebanon: A Study in Air Strategy," *Air University Review*, Vol. 16 (July–August 1965), p. 40.

2. Lieutenant Colonel Gary H. Wade, U.S. Army, *Rapid Deployment Logistics: Lebanon, 1958*, Research Survey 3 (Fort Leavenworth, Kan.: Combat Studies Institute, U.S. Army Command and General Staff College, October 1984), pp. 35, 37.

3. Roger J. Spiller, *"Not War but Like War": The American Intervention in Lebanon*, Leavenworth Paper 3 (Fort Leavenworth, Kan.: U.S. Army Command and General Staff College, January 1981), p. 51.

4. Bruce Palmer, *Intervention in the Caribbean* (Lexington: University Press of Kentucky, 1989), p. 148.

5. Ibid., p. 152.

6. Lawrence A. Yates, *Power Pack: U.S. Intervention in the Dominican Republic, 1965–1966*, Leavenworth Paper 15 (Fort Leavenworth, Kan.: U.S. Army Command and General Staff College, 1988), pp. 98–99.

7. U.S. Air Force, *Airlift in the Dominican Crisis*, Airborne Operations [2-3.7 AC.F]—Tab F (www.army.mil/cmh-pg/documents/abnops/tabf.htm [January 25, 2001]).

8. Dorothea Cypher, "Urgent Fury: The U.S. Army in Grenada," in Peter M. Dunn and Bruce W. Watson, eds., *American Intervention in Grenada: The Implications of Operation "Urgent Fury"* (Boulder, Colo.: Westview, 1985), p. 99; Gilbert S. Harper, "Logistics in Grenada: Supporting No-Plan Wars," *Parameters* (June 1990), p. 57.

9. Cypher, "Urgent Fury," pp. 99, 102. See also, Frank Uhlig Jr., "Amphibious Aspects of the Grenada Episode," in Dunn and Watson, *American Intervention*.

10. Lorenzo Crowell, "The Anatomy of Just Cause: The Forces Involved, the Adequacy of Intelligence, and Its Success as a Joint Operation," in Bruce W. Watson and Peter G. Tsouras, eds., *Operation Just Cause: The U.S. Intervention in Panama* (Boulder, Colo.: Westview, 1990), pp. 71, 76. See also, John W. Turner, "The Adequacy of Logistic Support," in Watson and Tsouras, *Operation Just Cause*, p. 124; Robert R. Ropelewski, "Planning, Precision, and Surprise Led to Panama Successes," *Armed Forces Journal International*, February 1990, pp. 26, 30.

11. Turner, "The Adequacy," pp. 124–25, reports that during the first two weeks 408 sorties airlifted 9,500 troops and 11,700 tons of cargo. Subtracting the first week's

totals leaves approximately 3,350 troops and 8,000 tons of cargo airlifted during the second week, or nearly 500 troops and 1,100 tons per day.

12. Crowell, "The Anatomy," pp. 93–94. *Cosmopolitan World Atlas* (Rand McNally, 1993), p. 274, cites a 1990 population for Panama City of 411,000, but a larger population of 770,000 including suburbs.

Appendix C

1. The dates for these statistics are respectively August 17, August 12, and August 1–2, 1994. Lieutenant General Daniel R. Schroeder, *Operation Support Hope 1994, After Action Report* (Headquarters, U.S. European Command, 1994), hereafter cited as *AAR*, p. 14, charts in appendix, and reprint of "Information Paper, Subject: Joint Task Force Support Hope Missions Identified by the National Command Authority and Key Advisers," August 13, 1994. At the beginning and end of Operation Support Hope, the bulk of sorties into Goma were NGO flights, which were contracted and scheduled by the UN High Commissioner for Refugees (UNHCR). At the peak of the operation, however, the overwhelming majority of sorties into Goma were U.S. aircraft. (4 C-141 x 20 tons) + (2 C-5 x 60 tons) = 200 tons/day.

2. The dates for these statistics are respectively August 17 and August 18–21, 1994. The 526 tons were carried on twenty-six U.S. and NGO sorties. Schroeder, *AAR*, charts in appendix; Lieutenant General Daniel Schroeder, USA (Ret.), interview with author, February 8, 1999. (5 C-141 x 20 tons) + (3 C-5 x 60 tons) + (6 C-130 x 20 tons) = 400 tons/day.

3. The dates for these statistics are August 5–7, 1994. Schroeder, *AAR*, charts in appendix; Schroeder, interview with author, February 8, 1999.

4. (8 C-141 x 20 tons) + (4 C-5 x 60 tons) = 400 tons/day. If the mix of aircraft were split evenly, the maximum daily capacity would be (6 x 20) + (6 x 60) = 480 tons.

5. Schroeder, *AAR*, reprint of "Memorandum for CINCEUR, Subject: Joint Task Force Support Hope Operational Concept Update Number 4," August 13, 1994.

6. Paul Jackson, *Jane's All the World's Aircraft* (Surrey: Jane's Information Group, 1995), pp. 565–66, reports that modern C-130s have a maximum payload of twenty-three to twenty-five tons, but twenty tons is more realistic.

7. Schroeder, *AAR*, pp. 16–18, charts in appendix; Schroeder, interview with author, February 8, 1999; Captain Robyn A. Chumley, "'Will You Please Pray for Us'—Relief for Rwandan Refugees," *Airman*, October 1994, p. 5. Tom Breen and Vago Muradian, "A Journey to Hell: The Air Force Is on the Move Again," *Air Force Times*, August 8, 1994, pp. 12–13.

Index